BETTER
THAN
DIVORCE

BETTER THAN DIVORCE

by

Ruthe T. Spinnanger

Logos International
Plainfield, New Jersey

Better Than Divorce
Copyright © 1978 by Logos International
All rights reserved
Printed in the United States of America
Library of Congress Catalog Card Number: 78-50751
International Standard Book Number: 0-88270-271-8
Logos International, Plainfield, New Jersey 07060

FOR

ALL CHILDREN OF DIVORCE

CONTENTS

Acknowledgments

Epigraphs from: *Dictionary of Thoughts*, Compiled by Tryon Edwards

Alcoholism: Based on notes from Alina Lodge, Rehabilitation Center, Blairstown, New Jersey

"Cry of the Blood": Fiction and truth recombined. *The Goddess* by Joyce Carol Oates

Preface

This book is based on situations in which, as a teacher, author, mother, and wife, I have been placed as counselor or confidante. People in conflict are often indiscriminate in dealing with their anxieties, and these essays are a direct outgrowth of circumstances which called for adaptation and understanding. It is no attempt to offer either simplistic cures or diagnoses. Rather, I have hoped to show the lifelong chain reactions of wasted potential that divorce sets in motion.

It is an intensely personal approach in which I have drawn upon a wide spectrum of subjects as well as case histories of people who, quite unknowingly, provided me with examples on which to base my emphasis. All have been given fictitious names, but I owe them a debt of gratitude for their invisible partnership in this book.

Golden-age couples who have remained married, and children who have been affected by divorce, have received far too little public, psychological or legal notice. Instead, we have focused on broken lives, and ignored the literal historic "proofs" of lives lived subjectively in the context of enduring marriage.

I have made no attempt to be systematic in my explorations, or to reinforce my point of view with scholarly references. What I have written I have interpreted on the basis of actual experience, and what is true for *one* individual may shed light on that complicated and collective organism we refer to as society, which is really a conglomeration of individuals.

No preface is complete without special thanks to my longtime friends, Alice Jane Foley and Bernice Johnson, who typed and deciphered my manuscript with utmost patience and unfailing encouragement.

BETTER
THAN
DIVORCE

Myth: Marriage as a Happiness Machine

*Only so far as a man is happily married
to himself, is he fit for married
life to another, and for family
life generally. (Novalis)*

It was a beautiful June day. In the rose garden of the large and stately home an anniversary party was in progress. Ladies in long dresses moved gracefully across the lawn while men in white slacks and navy blue blazers gathered in leisurely groups waiting to congratulate the couple whose golden wedding anniversary was being celebrated. A few guests were obviously discussing two cases of bitter divorce litigation. Details were passed around in social *sotto voce*, inasmuch as the man and woman being talked about were close relatives of the husband and wife in whose honor the party was being held.

Sentences were broken off, and there was a sudden separating of the intimate groups about the lawn, as a reporter and a photographer briskly made their way toward the receiving line for an on-the-scene interview. "And were you never tempted to divorce?" asked the reporter. "No," replied the gentle-looking, white-haired lady. "Only murder!"

What a placid acceptance of the fact that any day-piled-on-day, year-by-year intimacy will involve the entire spectrum of human feelings as well as virtues. Unfortunately, the never-never-land romances of stage and screen hold up mirrors to each extreme. We are shown either the heights of marital bliss or the most hair-raising aspects of marriage.

To move beyond divorce, one must meet every frustration with a creative empathy that is at once liberating and crisis-oriented, since to marry is to commit not merely one's heart and mind, but one's will. Consider empathy, that ability to put yourself in another person's place. Before one can so much as think along such lines, one must be set free from the domination of one's own feelings of anger, blame and frustration. Hence, to move beyond divorce is a liberating experience. I cannot control another, but I can refuse to be dominated by my own inner state, whatever that may be. It follows that one must be adaptable and flexible enough to see that any life, whether single, married, widowed, divorced, or so-called free love will inevitably involve some form of crisis. Deny it as we will, "Man is born to trouble as the sparks fly upward." The ancients were correct in that claim, and until we can reverse the laws of gravity this will be true for humans everywhere.

We cannot always change the circumstances which involve the most personal, the most intimate of disappointments, but we can control our responses to such agonies. Yet in the throes of anger and/or frustration, one does not feel love. At such time it is easy to conclude, "I never loved. I did not know what I was doing. I married in ignorance. I married too young. I married too hastily. I really didn't know what I was getting into." Innumerable, as well as devastatingly true, may be these rationales for divorce. But to act upon them is to take on a cycle of decisions based entirely on circumstance, and such decisions are as fluctuating as their foundations. Decisions were intended to reverse the order. Instead of being manipulated by our conditions, our decisions were meant to change the responses we let circumstances arouse. It is a question of will. The crisis-oriented approach does not nullify marriage; it merely alters the provocation which leads to the desire for escape.

First and foremost must be the decision not to decide anything in the clutches of any emotion! Test any and all emotions with the test of time and detachment. Cultivate calmness. (This is not unlike actual soil cultivation, in that it requires effort.) A crisis is a time for simple endurance. It is not a time to assess blame or update past failures. There must be a willingness to endure stress, which does not always mean resolving a crisis pleasantly. To be stoically pleasant is often a form of repression which merely delays the ultimate explosion. To endure involves a willingness to look at, and accept, the nonrational sides of one's own nature and that of one's mate. To endure means to accept family divergencies that run into multiplications of two times two, times four times four, until you are back to Adam and Eve.

Nor is the outcome final unity. After a crisis, anger, frustration, or anxiety, the after-calm can make individual differences acceptable and nonthreatening. This is what endurance means, and it is eminently worthwhile!

Cowardly? Masochistic? Not at all. To stay married is to opt for complexity; to settle for a lifetime of ambivalent feelings. "For better or for worse," are as much a part of divorce as they are of marriage. At the altar or at the judge's bench, one faces uncertainties with built-in factors of worse or better. Is it not wiser to "bear those ills we have, than fly to others that we know not of"? Whether one is married or not, there are no simple answers.

3

Marriage: Blame-Game or Power-Play?

. . . Joined for life
to strengthen each other in all labor,
to rest on each other in all sorrow,
to minister to each other in all pain,
to be one with each other in silent,
unspeakable memories at the moment
of that last parting. (George Eliot)

For centuries a favorite marriage myth has been variations on the theme of "happily ever after." In this way the path of pure love has been liberally strewn with sleeping princesses, dragons to be slain, and pumpkin coaches, until the final union of whatever romantic pair we might choose brings the implication that once together, fairy-tale love would defeat all obstacles. If such were not enough, there are volumes upon volumes of autobiographical proof that marital love *has* overwhelmingly triumphed in the face of unbelievable odds. In short, divorce was rare when fairy tales were believed. But perhaps it was not actual belief that aided in keeping the married united for life. Rather, it may have been a complex network of social traditions, built-in taboos, lack of opportunity, secrecy, repression, pride, lack of communication, lack of economic mobility, and lack of marketable skills for women which kept marriages intact. One can cite the example of George Eliot, whose real name was Marianne Evans, and for whom neither traditions nor taboos were determinative; where social isolation, secrecy and repression were overthrown; and where women sold their skills and lives under male pseudonyms for freedom from marriage. These examples have given us the fabric of exceptions—fascinating lives which were, indeed, stranger than fiction.

However, it is not to the broken marriages or to the self-emancipated that we must address ourselves if we wish to examine alternatives to, or marital conditions beyond, divorce. We must remain close to the side of the golden anniversary set.

We must set aside all stereotyped notions that the aged have "forgotten." Behind the wrinkles of age, very few people are mentally and emotionally older than the mid-thirties. In physique, in judgment, in patience, and in endurance and ambition, the differences may be vast, but in memory there are remembrances that are eternally marked "today." True, they may be gilded over with a mind-set of optimism, or melancholy nostalgia, whatever the individual's temperament decrees. Nevertheless, the incontrovertible evidence for remaining married is the document of years which cannot be erased, regardless of emotional "coloring."

Did they elope? Were they engaged for a long period? Were they very young? Were they poor? Were they middle-class? Were they rich? None of these variables are necessary basics for clues to the key for fifty years of married life.

In spite of religious difference, we know that one of the cornerstone values current fifty years ago was *truth*; it was the cement of society itself, broadly speaking. As a moral value, truth's mode of application differed greatly from that of today. Then, it was fundamental and absolute—today, truth is relative and many-leveled.

Being absolute, truth had for its offspring, love, and for its foundation, duty. Without love, truth becomes a despot and

6

an instrument for persecution, just as love would be weak and vacillating without truth. Yet both truth and love are worthless unless they are translated into action. These were the ideals with which our present-day, golden-anniversary couples entered marriage. The love and truth they had subscribed to in their most romantic moments were seen as the truths by which they must live in all the days to follow.

Did they meet with opposition? Were they angry, irritated, disappointed with each other and the circumstances of their life together? Of course! Human nature has not changed, for all its present sophistication. When history labels the twentieth century the most violent century in the history of man, it will do so on the basis of its parallel "burden." This is the "burden" of accumulated rational, materialistic, and technological advances, which have done nothing to erase or mitigate the original depravity of man. Although every *opinion* of men or science would direct us away from this truth, we have only to flick a button on our television sets and another on our reclining chairs to see the harvest of violence which is witlessly employed to beget violence *with* profit! Again, we cannot simplistically relate the increase in violence to any one single development or invention. Yet we cannot ignore the powerful connection between what enters the eye and what is translated into action. Ever since the Edenic beauty of the apple, the *seen* has been reacted to, and acted upon. It is much more difficult to change into imagery the abstractions of truth, love and duty.

Granting, then, that marriage of fifty years ago involved the same impulses to passion, temper, love-hate ambiguities, where these existed, why did they stay *with* it?

Among those long married, the enlightened brought a healthy distrust for the permanence of feelings. They accepted the fact that the human heart is deceitful above all things; they knew those feelings would inevitably fluctuate.

Therefore, they added to a natural preference for each other, the insurance of commitment, a *will* to make the marriage endure. There would be no easy outs. In this they created a double guarantee of success, since head as well as heart were in command.

However, not all the will in the world can rule both heart and head without a dynamic stronger than human inclinations. And who will dare deny that there are not situations in any marriage which arouse inclinations that are no more than civilized impulses to murder, covered over with a thin veneer of self-control? As one wife said in an outburst of pent-up rage, "See that plant stand? That's how I broke his arm and it's damn lucky I didn't have a knife!" She believes her divorce is based entirely on his failures, as all her legal papers indicate. Rarely does anyone in a divorce action examine *his own* murderous impulses. Rather than face up to a personal lack of self-control, and grow up to be inner-directed people, couples find it easier to join the blame-game and power-play of the divorce courts.

Under the old value system, will power had as its most powerful ally, a strong sense of duty. A bleak prospect? By no means. In practical daily requirements, it was believed that the nearest duty was the duty of today; that done, power would always be given for the next duty. Does this prove painful or rewarding? To a generation schooled for immediate gratification, it is odious. In experience and experiment, a duty performed becomes a heady moral tonic. Through fulfilling the claims of the day, the "must" that we all humanly reject in the word *duty* turns miraculously into an invigorating, "I can!"

Whatever lies ahead, the consciousness of having done one's best in the line of duty may seem a laughable satisfaction to a pleasure-motivated world, but it carries with it a wealth of good humor and cheerfulness, as well as strength for mind and heart.

How to Disagree Agreeably

*The last word is the most infernal and
dangerous of machines, and the husband
and wife should no more fight to get it
than they would struggle for possession
of a lighted bombshell. (Jerrold)*

"Why can't you take your butter from the end of the cube?" says Ralph to his wife irritably. A precision engineer, Ralph loves details, and the exactitude of figures fascinate him. His wife does not. Like many creative people, her hands may be in the dishpan, but her heart is constantly on the wing. In a thousand little ways she manages to irritate her husband. Should she adapt? Should she make every effort to change her ways? Should she reason that in smoothing away this minor annoyance she will be helping herself? Surely it is a small concession for her to cease from digging her butter out from the middle of the cube and take it neatly and precisely from the end? Clearly, the butter cube is not the real issue. Irritability will merely find another focus. If it is not the butter, it will be something else.

Before long, whether the husband criticizes the wife, or the wife the husband, the target of whatever the disagreement will become indignant. The opposing view will be seen as "unfair."

Even more devastating are the justifiable disagreements. When a mate has actually failed in some area, the other will be tempted to *use* the very real failure as a verbal weapon, or if not as a weapon, as a defense mechanism. What then? No one is more familiar with our anxieties, our self-criticisms, than the person with whom we live. And no one can reach a marriageable age without encountering a few failures and defeats. It is easy then for a mate to turn a painful memory into an occasion for ego-mutilation. The buried humiliation is updated. If this is done too often the failure becomes an obsession, either with the mate who finds it a handy final thrust, or the mate at whom it is directed.

In the human areas of defeat, the most common area of ego-deflation in marriage concerns money. A wife with her days at home finds time to pore over "picture-book" home furnishings, or listens to the media tell her that she is made for "better" things than homemaking and child-rearing. Thus her thinking is directed to the *wish-level* of existence. As she mindlessly makes beds, loads the dishwasher, irons, bakes or whatever, her mind revolves around *things*. She plots and schemes for ways and means to have better things, to redecorate, refurnish, remake, rearrange, remove, and finally, to re-activate her husband's ambition for more money. Meantime, in the real world of business, the husband looks forward to home as the one place where he can lay competition aside. Instead, he is more intimately exposed. Every familiar item is portrayed as inferior or obsolete The wife's wish-syndrome knows no bounds once it is unleashed. In attacking a man's skill as a provider, the wife can do irrevocable harm. The husband becomes hostile, then bitter, and may finally lose all confidence in himself. The loss of many a man's job is the systematic destruction of his self-image in a relationship which must, by the nature of its intimacy, nurture or destroy.

On the other hand, men are equally adept at finding the wife's failure signposts. One wife whose mother had been twice divorced had deeply resolved that, unlike her mother, she would make her marriage endure. In moods of self-dissatisfaction, it was easy for the husband to project his own ego-insecurities by the incessant water-on-stone-method of saying, "You're just like your mother!" In spite of the fact that her mother had many fine qualities, the wife saw this as rejection. An analyst would recognize the husband's words as a "way" out of some personal frustration, but a wife ordinarily reacts. In this instance, the wife set out to prove her husband wrong.

In both cases there is a blockage of some important desire. When a wife complains of money, the husband is made to feel he has not "measured up." This may not be based on *actual* inadequacy, but on the false evaluation of *wishful* standards by the wife. Likewise, the husband who compares his wife unfavorably with her mother touches the "Achilles' heel" of her insecurity, the secret fear that she will identify with her mother's defeats. She feels she *should* be different. Can such apparently deep-rooted differences be lived with amicably? Suppose the wife really believes the husband could earn more money? Suppose the husband dislikes his wife's mother intensely and faces a daily reminder in what he sees as a resemblance in his wife? In each case, the truth is as he or she sees it.

Facts and figures can be brought to bear on the wife's version of her truth, and behavior patterns could be traced to the satisfaction of the husband's beliefs, yet nothing would be solved or altered by so doing.

To retaliate for an unacceptable truth is merely to add fuel to the fires of resentment. By reacting, one is allowing the mate's idea of truth to dictate how one will feel and what one will do. This is to be dependent on unrealistic expectations which may be true for someone else and false for you.

Each partner must resolve at the outset that, despite the intimacy of the relationship, neither one *owes* the other anything! There can be no "how-to" rules in marriage where spontaneity is a built-in buttress. Just as the intricacies of our legal system are unknown to the law-abiding, just so should be any idea of "would-should" in a marriage. National law is a "schoolmaster." It is there to remind us of the broken law. Similarly, marriage *rules* do not exist until corrective action must be taken, and then it is often too late.

To look upon one's marriage partner as a debtor dooms any marriage. We give to the *other* the self that we actually *are*. We may say that in loving we love not the other, but the self we become when we are together. As the poem states it, "I love you, not only for what you are, but for what I am when I am with you." Therefore, in mutual interaction, I shall not change you nor expect you to change for me. I shall have one obligation: to be the *best me* I can become. In so doing, I shall remember that what you may dislike in me does not lie in my person, or the events of our marriage, or circumstances, but in our individual reactions.

Yet how will I accomplish the task of not reacting to an idea or accusation which I find wholly unacceptable? By directing my entire attention on these anxious, fearful, irritable, or hostile sources of marital disagreement, I will become so involved in studying cause and effect that where reaction, angry reaction, was once a response, it will be displaced by a stronger idea. Since only ideas can replace ideas, by examining causes of disagreement, which is by no means easy or automatic, I will refuse to be dominated by my own unthinking responses and/or resentments. But neither response or resentment can be uprooted by will power. However, they can be displaced and dispersed through other ideas. Within the framework of marriage, this is what is meant by becoming "my own person."

The focus of attention must be drawn away from mutual differences. It must be seen that the differences which were so attractive when feelings ran high have a way of changing in the day-to-day repetitions of marriage. Why did we get along in the early days of our marriage, when we disagree about nearly everything now? There is a simple answer, which is by no means simplistic. We got along *because we wanted to!*

4

On Being Crisis-Oriented

*He that will not apply new remedies
must expect new evils. (Bacon)*

Very few people marry without some feelings of intensity.
In the one and same relationship, there are built-in benefits
and limitations. Commitment and responsibility impose
restrictions on the life we are investing in another. But
perhaps the greatest danger arises from our approach to the
benefits of marriage, because to these we bring virtually
airborne castles of expectancy.

Instead of reality, expectation becomes the foundation
upon which we build, and when our wishes fail to
materialize, we harbor hard thoughts about our mates and
the marriage relationship itself, for failing to gratify our
expectations. Instead of rejecting, examining, or analyzing
our expectations, we replace the old wishes with new ones
and begin a new cycle of futile expectations. Yet marital
success and safety lie in expecting one thing: that *change* is
an inevitable part of existence.

Is this a bleak prospect? By no means. To reject our
expectations is not to advocate a masochistic acceptance of

what pains or disappoints us. Rather, it is understanding that our very expectations are subject to change and therefore, adaptable.

What, exactly, is a crisis? Any development which calls for a response to change is a crisis. It need not be threatening, it may not be catastrophic, but whether major or minor, whether from people or events, change is taking place in the life and critical readjustments are called for.

Laudable as they may be, high expectations may have a damaging, built-in rigidity—an all or nothing basis. On the other hand, we cannot afford to weaken ourselves with any presupposing "ifs." To say of a mate, of children, or circumstances, "If such a thing happens, I just *know* I couldn't stand it," is to sell yourself short. You cannot measure anything you may do in the future by what you have done in the past. To do so is to set limits that will, paradoxically, be self-defeating and self-fulfilling. You will cut off, in advance, untapped sources of strength, and yes, you *will* fulfill your own words and not be able to measure up.

Condition yourself for crisis and catastrophe! Not fearfully, but deliberately. However, conditioning yourself to take whatever comes does not mean that you merely exchange your unrealistic expectations of "pie-in-the-sky," or equivalents thereof, for an equally unrealistic catalogue of fears. What is recommended, through testing, is that in meditative or relaxed moments, ask yourself, experimentally, "What would I do if. . . ?" This is a far different "if" than to say, "I can't stand it!" This is the positive approach of, "What would I do?" The emphasis is on *action*, for *doing*, in the worst of catastrophes.

The first act in any crisis is acceptance. Not simply assenting to the fact that you are caught in a set of circumstances from which there may be no escape; an *act* is called for. Whether the phone rings at two o'clock in the morning, or you awake with a fast-beating heart and an extrasensory perception of impending catastrophe, the prescribed *act* can be the same.

Let us consider the record of an actual phone call at two o'clock. "This is the police. You are wanted in the emergency room at the hospital." Half asleep, you gasp, "What has happened?" You look in the driveway and see that your son's car is missing. The voice at the other end of the phone says soothingly, "Your son has been in an accident. He is in no danger, but you are wanted at the hospital." Rain is pouring down, and you must go alone. You block out the extrasensory knowledge that your son has been killed. You refuse to accept it, and attribute it to broken sleep, night fears, and natural exaggerations induced by stormy weather.

What, in fact, is to be done in similar or worse circumstances? There are guidelines that have been tested and found never to have failed. A large claim? Yes.

How had she reached the hospital? Recklessly? No, the old guidelines had once again proved their worth. Out of context, her mind was filled with words that infused calmness as if by literal transfusion to her fast-beating heart. She wondered irrelevantly if that was the way in which Joan of Arc's "voices" had spoken to her. She heard herself repeating, "God is our refuge and strength. . . . Therefore will not we fear, though the earth be removed, and though the mountains be carried into the midst of the sea" (Ps 46:1-2). At that point, the words reminded her of the San Andreas Fault in California. "What if that part of the state were, in actual fact, 'carried into the midst of the sea'?" And there, driving through a rain-darkened night, she forgot for a brief moment her own fear-filled errand, and prayed for the well-being of others.

Keeping time with the rhythm of the windshield wipers, she repeated rote-fashion, the very words she had been forced to memorize as a child, "Therefore will not we fear, . . . Though the waters thereof roar and be troubled, though the mountains shake with the swelling thereof" (Ps. 46:2-3).

She noticed she was not driving fast; her hands were easy on the wheel; her heart had ceased racing. Memory carried her on, "God is in the midst of her; she shall not be moved: God shall help her, and that right early" (v. 5). At the word "early" she managed a wry smile and thought, "But I didn't expect this at two in the morning."

Walking from her car to the hospital, she found herself murmuring, "The LORD of hosts is with us; the God of Jacob is our refuge" (Ps. 46:7). Her fears proved true. Her son had been killed instantly. Bending over his broken body, the next stanza came. "Come, behold the works of the LORD, what desolations he hath made in the earth" (Ps. 46:8). There was no reproach that this was God's fault, and as the deep wracking sobs came, she could not explain afterwards whether the fact of death, or the words, "The LORD gave, and the LORD hath taken away; blessed be the name of the LORD" (Job 1:21) had loosed the floodgates of her tears.

Much later, in that long leisure which follows death, she was able to move on to the comfort of the tenth verse of Psalm 46, "Be still, and know that I am God. . . . I will be exalted in the earth."

But what of the person for whom such words have no meaning? How are their problems to be met?

The first step in any crisis is to recognize and avoid self-pity. Misfortune becomes a double burden when we bemoan our catastrophes by turning them over and over in our minds, asking that most futile of all questions, "Why me?"

The second step is to transmute problems, whether small or great. All troubles may be allegorically likened to rocky or desert land, unfit for flowers, fruit or grain. The land can be abandoned, or it can be cultivated and struggled with, until it yields what the ancients described: " . . . the desert shall rejoice, and blossom as the rose" (Isa. 35:1). The same is no less true of our human lives, and autobiographies of disadvantaged humans are filled with the truths of it. Those "rocks" in the "soil" of our human lives are a call to *do*, to *act*, to *resist!*

Resist what? First, the temptation to inaction; to paralyzed, repetitive mulling over and over of the problem. It may be said, "I've tried that, and it doesn't work! In fact, I've tried everything!"

There are problems for which we all recognize there are no cures: death, terminal disease, crippling handicaps. Where these are met in ways that evoke our admiration, it is usually due to a profoundly simple cause. That cause is *change of emphasis*. It is a reorientation of one's entire pattern of thinking. No one has ever said it is easy. It must be a stern aim, taken on with purpose and belief in its efficacy, that is, with conscious effort.

Like a regimen of physical exercises, the conscious aim does not become habitual apart from daily renewal of a changed emphasis. Moreover, a changed emphasis cannot be altogether willed. St. Augustine said in his *Confessions*, "The mind will not obey the mind." But the mind will respond to other ideas when it is willingly exposed to other patterns of thought. For many, this exposure finds its dynamic in the ways of faith. The command, ". . . be ye transformed by the renewing of your mind," (Rom. 12:2) implies a continuing process of renewal.

If computers must be fed a program to produce a given result, the human mind, which is a far more complicated computer, designed to deal with *different* programming each day, must be fed a new emphasis for each new day's failure or success.

It will be noted that a computer and the human mind may, indeed, be fed a new emphasis each day, but unlike the computer, the mind is attached to human emotions. In spite of the fact that a mental attitude can be "programmed" and "conditioned" to such a degree that one can cite the old cliche, "It's not *what* happens to you, it's *how* you take it." Nevertheless, emotions will come. Events will bring about a physical reaction, and all the feelings that spell out loss of control will cry for attention in the forms of accelerated heartbeat, tears, trembling, tightness across the chest, numbness, stomach pains, tiredness, lightheadedness. These are entirely natural reactions, but in the very midst of their domination it is possible to fight for *self*-control. It is possible to summon determination, and after the first moment of crisis search your own heart for that *previously* adopted attitude, "I *will* make the best of this!"

Since change is inevitable in every life, *practice* changing your plans, your daily routine, your expectations, anything, so long as you learn to deal with every variation of crisis, every extreme or decisive change.

The person who will train himself for crisis must learn to keep the capacity for effort alive through exercise. According to William James one achieves this by being systematic in unnecessary deprivations every day. He says, ". . . do every day or two something for no other reason than that you would rather not do it, so that when the hour of dire need draws nigh, it may find you not unnerved and untrained to stand the test. Asceticism of this sort is like insurance which a man pays on his house and goods. The tax does him no good at the time, and possibly may never bring him a return. But if the fire does come, his having paid it will be his salvation from ruin. So with the man who has daily inured himself to habits of concentrated attention, energetic volition, and self-denial in unnecessary things. He will stand like a tower when everything rocks around him, and when his softer fellow-mortals are winnowed like chaff in a blast."

5

Invisible Child Abuse

The difference between brutal and visible
abuse and subtle but invisible abuse is
the difference between being bruised by
beatings and killed by poison.

The marital quarrel is tapering off. In a parting verbal spar the wife throws a bundle at her husband descending the stairs. "Here, take your—!" In a quick reflexive action, the husband catches the object being thrown at him. It is a small child. There will be no visible marks on the little body, but the scars on the far more vulnerable soul will remain, beyond seeing and therefore beyond healing.

Little wonder that Khrushchev could claim that Russia would bury America without firing a single bullet! With one in every three marriages ending in divorce, we would do well to examine this unheralded battleground which carries no picturesque cross. Indeed, we will do it by means of our weakest link—the home.

Meantime, we allow all forms of mass media to pander to our love for a myth: the fantasy that successful marriage is a romantic affair. Marriage with anyone is hard work, in which romance must inevitably take on the qualities of dailiness. And, as if one myth were not enough in this

American battleground, we add that fake criterion for human behavior, the thought that happiness determines all, while duty, which carries happiness as a by-product, is a forgotten concept.

Forgotten, also, are the children, those small prisoners in whom every detail of their parents' lives leave imprints, the invisible scars of terror. The child's sense of familiarity and comfort from the parents, which is associated with continuity and sameness, is broken by divorce. The wife often goes to her mother, and at least two other families are drawn into the battleground. Do these supposedly thinking adults realize that the child never sees the offending mate through adult eyes?

Remember the book, *A Tree Grows In Brooklyn*? It is the sensitive, drunken father who is immortalized by unchanging love from his children, not the hardworking mother. Why is this so often true of small children? Because they sense the undercurrents of irritability and resentment which emanate from the working parent. For children there is no problem of reactions that arouse guilt. They saw his cheerfulness with no knowledge of its alcoholic source. On the contrary, the mother was no doubt as disturbed by her own reactions to the drinking as she was to the actions it aroused, and the deprivations it set in motion. Her indignation and self-pity are far more offensive in the eyes of small uncomprehending children than a raucous, laughing, deliriously singing, drunken father. Above all, it is the child's eye view and needs that should be consulted. Instinct is always a truer guide to the sickness of alcohol than cold reason.

But no enduring pattern exists for the children of divorce. According to Erik Erickson in *Childhood and Society*, enduring patterns are needed if the child is to have a basis for self-identity, which later gives him a sense of being "all right." Instead, grandparents, who should know better, plant the enduring seeds of guilt and self-doubt by referring to the missing parent in derogatory terms. For example, the phone rings and grandma tells her daughter, "Here's that no-good husband of yours!" Does she know that a child translates this into adult guilt for *any* love he or she feels? The child loves both grandma and the missing parent, but has no inner resources to deal with the dilemma of a divided heart. Fight or flight, passivity or rage (reactions to a reality we cannot cope with) will be the result. He may never verbalize, in his formative years, his deep sense of "I'm not O.K." Many years may have to pass before this is projected on a world which betrayed his early trust before he is able to say in violent terms, "You're not O.K. either!"

As Khrushchev said, "Not a single bullet needs to be fired!"

When children from such homes bring their sick self-images to adulthood, we will remember that history is never past; it stalks the present moment. We will remember that our decadence brought us the prophecy, "Not a single bullet needs to be fired!" Our defeat will be from within, from the very nucleus of our nation: the home.

We may erect our child-care centers until every woman is free to leave her home, but we can never escape the responsibility which makes us human. Until the needs of children are given first priority we have failed in that responsibility. Equal rights for women can never, without courting disaster, precede the needs of children. Children, who can lift no voice in their own defense, are the silent seed-bed for a future of violence and anger that we are seeing in increasingly frequent atrocities committed by our youth. Meantime, we are our children's keepers! If there are no visible marks by which to tally their "abuse" it does not follow that none exists. The wounds that carry no marks are far more difficult to eradicate, for "who can pluck from the heart a rooted sorrow?"

6

Calendar of Catastrophe

Parents repeat their lives in their offspring.
(R. Palmer)

She will be four years old Saturday, and I have watched her grow old. Old? No, not in terms of chronology, but old in the guardianship of a divided heart. Once, she felt free to shout in joy-filled abandon, "Daddy! My daddy!" as she ran into his outstretched arms. The first time I saw it, I noted the jealousy suffusing her mother's face and groaned silently, "Oh, no!" But my foreboding fear came true. The divorce is in progress.

And that warm-hearted little four-year-old has learned to check her spontaneity. Anxiously, she seeks to justify the collapse of what was once her world. Over and over in her play she puts a toy soldier into bed; she says yes when I ask if that is her daddy. She is too eager for approval. She strives in all her baby ways to compensate for a nameless pain. Unable to account for absence, she is invisibly chained to a loss she dares not name. Moreover, there is a larger ache that words will never appease for those "other" words screamingly flung over her listening little head.

Subconsciously, her nightmare "cries in the night" plead to be allowed to love equally! Divorce is aging for little girls.

When I admire a gift her daddy has given her, saying "Who gave you that?" she glances uneasily at her mother and answers listlessly in subdued, unchildlike tones, "It's just a present." A woman's intuitive wisdom, too soon bestowed, is in her answer. But her tongue betrays her carefulness when daddy comes to visit. Involuntarily, without intent, the words slip out, "Can daddy stay for dinner?" Her mother is firm, and hastily the young father saves the awkward pause by saying, "Daddy has had his supper." (He does not mention that alimony fare is a hamburger.)

Am I asking for an end to divorce? By no means. I am begging that mothers who have every legitimate ground for divorce should make every effort to see their mates through the eyes of their children, that they would remember the world dimensions of a child, especially a very small child, are father and mother!

Does the agony of the child last? After counseling scores of teen-age girls, I hear that little four-year-old at age sixteen tell me, "We listened to every car, every beep of a horn, to every tick of a clock, and my father used to come every Sunday, but my mother made it so bad for him that he stopped coming." It would seem that liberation in both sexes may now be translated into the self-surrounded self. It is a dead-end concept. Childbirth should awake a commitment to consider, think, and above all, to *feel for the feelings of these inarticulate little ones.*

HUNGER

A little girl boasts hopefully,
"See, mommy?
I ate all my food!"
Eager for approval
To pacify her nameless pain,
Unable to account for absence,
And invisibly chained to loss,
She dares not name that larger ache,
Will never find
Words that can bridge
Those screamingly flung
Over her listening, glistening little head.

The self-surrounded self,
Her alter ego
Will never hear
The shy, involuntary heart-cry,
"Can daddy stay for dinner?"

7

"Cry of the Blood"

. . . I will lead on softly, according as
. . . the children be able to endure.
(Gen. 33:14)

Some part of Julia had never grown beyond the age of six.
Although she was sixty-six years old, she could still see her
father's last good-bye. In those days they did not tell their
children that mommy and daddy were going to get a divorce.
It was easier to say they were going to the farm for the
summer while daddy worked in town. She had totally
blocked out the author of that nagging question, "Who do
you love most, daddy or mommy?" Which one of them had
asked her that? Or had a lawyer asked it?

She remembered a six-year-old's reply, "I love you both
the same." She was eager to please, careful not to offend. A
series of welfare homes had followed the visit to the farm.
No doubt the court was deciding which parent was best
suited to be both mother and father. And so she was left with
the memory of her father walking away from them at the
railroad station. No word had been said about permanence,
yet she remembered the terrible cry in her heart, "Papa!
Papa! Come back!" No sound had escaped; she would *will*

him to return, but he had walked away with a high, lifted head. And for the rest of a long life, in one way or another, she would be calling for papa.

For another little boy and girl it had begun another way. The firm that employed Jimmy's father had decreed that a five-month's refresher course in a distant city would be mandatory. Jimmy was not quite a year old and his sister Suzy would be three. During that separation (a common practice on the part of corporations) Jimmy's mother had decided to begin divorce proceedings. All except the father agreed it would be best for the children. Certainly it would be better to have one parent than two who fought constantly. Far better to separate before the attachment became too deep; young children forget easily.

If they were anything, the children were better behaved than their playmates from unbroken homes. There seemed no evidence of any traumatic experience in either child. True, Suzy was very protective of little Jimmy, but that was viewed as no more than a big sister's way with little brothers. "Were they not mothers who are babies still?" However, when Jimmy was three, his mother had a sudden change of heart and invited Jimmy's daddy for Christmas Eve. "Let us put up the tree and assemble the toys. You can sleep with Jimmy and be in the house when the children awake on Christmas Day."

All that night a little hand would reach out and a small boy's voice would ask over and over, "Are you there, daddy?" Not once did he say what most little boys were saying that night, "Will Santa be here when I wake up?" No, the biggest thought, conscious or subconscious, had been, "Are you there, daddy?"

There. That is how a child spells mom and dad. T-H-E-R-E! Near enough for little hands to reach out and touch; for all little fingers to nestle in the large, circled palm of daddy's warm hand. It was more than a touch. It was a deep unutterable need, a *daily* need in which to learn that the world is a safe place.

Years passed, and daddy's absence became a pattern to which the children appeared well adjusted. Jimmy's mother was pleased that the children's progress was always a safe topic of conversation. "How are your adorable children? Is Suzy still the darling of all her teachers? Jimmy also? Such brilliant and beautiful children!"

But when Jimmy was eleven he refused to attend school. Suzy, thirteen, ran away from home, then, frightened, turned herself in at a nearby police station. Jimmy, once eager for school, and filled with accounts of the day's triumphs, would awake refusing to attend school. His stomach ached, or his head ached, or he had not slept from nightmares. His mother with her own job deadline would phone frantically for a sitter. Other times, he would keep her awake because he was unable to sleep. Like a much younger child, he would crawl into her bed, crying hysterically about his bad dreams; hiding his face in the pillow next to hers; pressing his back against her. Again, he would scream for her in the night, afraid even to leave his bed. She would speak calmly, repeating soothing comfort, offering him her own sleeping pills, assuring him she would not leave him even if he fell asleep. Anxiety became her way of life. Would he outgrow this?

The counselor, brought in as a result of Suzy's police episode, now saw Jimmy also. Mother's anxiety became a free-floating contagion. The family mood became a nightmarish cycle of loss of control. Both children fastened onto the mother's anxiety, which had its roots in unacknowledged guilt. She found herself reviewing the steps that had led to her divorce. No, there had been no way she could have kept her marriage going. But she would reach her conclusion only to begin again. Her mental obsession, never verbalized to the children, nonetheless communicated itself to them. They began questioning her accusingly. "Where is dad? Why doesn't he come to visit us any more? You hated him, didn't you? You hate us too, don't you?" The counselor maintained impartial sessions with all three, but no amount of wisdom can relieve a child's recognition of an amputated home. No surrogate father image, however well liked, can replace absence in the ordinary dailiness of life. Regardless of how common divorce becomes, as long as there are enduring marriages, a child senses the "wrongness" of his own broken home. Moreover, even a very young child is not exempt from the "cry of the blood" for his *real* father.

Little Jimmy's repeated question, "Are you there, daddy?" which was more important to him than thoughts of Santa or toys has been deliberately referred to here as a "cry of the blood." Theories of affection may differ; some will say it is acquired, others will say it is innate. If it is acquired, Jimmy's love for dad and mom is little different than the cupboard love of a cat and dog for its master, and based on no more than the satisfactions they bring him. A close observation of Jimmy's growth and development reveals that the father who was removed from him first by corporate decree (because his job training and salary depended on such a removal), and secondly by divorce, in no way lessened his attachment to his father. The craving for affection, for nearness, for continuity, for predictability, for simple *thereness* was not based on a granted satisfaction, but on *denial* of these gratifications. But our entire view of human nature and of the family and children will be profoundly changed if we see human love as no more than a by-product of parental treatment.

The divorcing parent who is indifferent to the child's need

for the missing mate is granting a right to himself that is tantamount to child rejection. In spite of every provision for the child's physical needs, and in spite of his own affection for the child, the single parent cannot meet the child's need for dual identification with both father and mother. While intensive studies have been undertaken to study the consequences of infant deprivation, techniques for measuring the full range of human development in children of divorce lags behind perhaps by virtue of the daily occurrence of divorce. Yet the fact that divorce has become so common that it is no longer regarded as a shame or a disgrace, in no way nullifies the effect on the children involved. Entirely omitted from divorce proceedings is the child's perception of his parents. In cases where children *are* consulted, an expert is often called in. Seldom are such decisions the result of the two parents' own observations of their children's needs. The fact that children *are* consulted in a divorce case is most frequently the result of one parent's desire to obtain full custody rather than shared custody. Obviously a *true* perception of the parent by the child would have to take into account the mixed emotions that are aroused when denial or correction or moderate discipline is administered. Also, a child's view of parental restriction is a variable that changes as he grows from one stage to another in his development. Much will depend on his own need to admire or to rebel, and even such views are influenced by the passing of time, until the conflicting desires that remembrances set in motion are solidified by an adult mind-set of negativism or idealization. The safest course for children is for mother and father to be a microcosm of that larger, outside world, where they may resist the restraints of two united people and have a proving ground for the testing of their own abilities and rights in the limited world of a united home.

RETARDED LOVE

He must not love
The hated loved one.
Escaping from his crib,
Flung over cradled bars
By his Amazonian
Amazing mother,
He learns resistance.
Climbing out again,
Again, again, again,
He learns persistence.

Behind repeatedly closed doors
He hears in the hum
Of an electric razor,
His silent father's voice.

He must try another way.
Head-down in infant anguish,
Shaping the comforting sound,
He moans himself to sleep.
Dad-N? Dad-N? Dad-N?

He will forget.
Un-blooded surrogates
Will leech themselves
To his mood-driven mother.
A man he will become;
Programed to pain
From the world-woman's hand;
Programed to intervene
Between desire and denial

From his mother's breast
He learns, too early to unlearn,
That there are other ways.

8

The "New" American Slavery

A man without religion is to be pitied,
but a godless woman is a horror above
all things. (Miss Evans)

We do not recognize our most recent American slaves because there are no picturesque blocks on which they are sold. There is no auctioneer to point out their value. There are no distinctions of color, race or creed whereby we may recognize them. There are no ads whereby the purchaser may pick and choose the merchandise of another human being. However, if we accept the usual definition of slavery, we know that they are human beings owned and dominated by other humans.

Are they women? By no means. In spite of all the shrill, feminist cries of "Unfair and discriminatory!" women have never lacked wiles or weal to protest our woes. If we have not ruled the world in name, we have ruled it, willingly or unwillingly, by way of the cradle. Our babes have learned their life-directions largely from the hands that rocked those cradles, whether we will acknowledge that fact or not. That this fact may be fair or unfair is beside the point. The time is long past due when we should recognize that life by its very nature *as* life is unfair. Life can never, by any form of government, grant the same quantity, size, value, rights, abilities, strength or rank to human beings. No, much as we might dramatize, publicize and bemoan male and female inequities, we are not slaves!

Our new slaves are a large segment of our population who are mostly without legal representation, and who, through dependency, and totally without choice, are under the power and domination of others. I refer to preschool children from broken homes. These little ones are the loveless slaves of adults whose emotions have blinded them to the real meaning of love: a concern for the well-being of another, in these cases, their children. Whatever the rationale, such adults decide that divorce is the only solution to what is (more often than not) an inability to tolerate their own projections, i.e. themselves.

We may describe such children as pawns of the marital power-play, a "possession" of whichever partner displays the most "power." Or, they are the "money" that can be squeezed from legal squadrons and titled nontaxable "child-support." Again, they may be regarded as no more than mere property.

There is no document that parallels the divorce decree for children. Their legal disposition carries no ticket to freedom or any act of manumission. The law provides protection for numerous injuries, but none for the permanently damaged divided hearts of little ones who innocently ask, "Can daddy stay for supper?" or, "Where does daddy sleep?" The anxiety and insecurity behind such questions, the denials of childlike trusting love are cruelly dismissed with such sweeping generalizations as, "Kids forget so easily. Kids are very adaptable." And all this is said in spite of what we know about early "patterning." For generations we have traced, biographically and genetically, the ineradicable effect of "conditioning" from age zero to seven in grown-up adults, yet we continue to permit—worse, *propagate*—a slavery which is no less virulent for being without a label and, therefore, invisible.

For generations we have seen what visible slavery did to our nation and to those who were its victims, but are we prepared to face similar reactions in children from broken homes? These are children who are often placed in "institutional storage" with no continuity in their relationship with their original mothers and fathers. What has the family tie granted them? Often parents so absorbed in their own interest that the child is virtually an emotional exile. The seeds of mistrust are planted and the interaction from which the child should build his own sense of identity is shattered. Being a "slave" to a parent's emotional self-absorption at a stage when his own sense of self is not even formed will later develop into a pervasive "behind the scenes" hatred.

Will future psychiatic help provide a measure of help for these children? Too often treatment and cure builds on previous relationships and where there is no record of loving relationship with nurturing adults how can they relate to a person with whom their only relationship is in talk or play "therapy"? Success in psychiatric techniques is tied to certain conditions which are lacking in many children from broken homes, that is, the need for cooperation with the parents, in which the parents show a willingness to, also, go into treatment themselves. Without such cooperation there can be no carry-over into everyday life.

9

Lawless Ladies Protected by Law

The future of society is in the hands of mothers; if the world was lost through woman she alone can save it. (Beaufort)

"And if I have my way, he'll never *see* these children!" So goes a mother's power-play, spoken in bitterness and anger. Who knows what concealed frustrations and/or justifications such words imply? Certainly no lawyer, psychologist or judge, however skilled, can accurately assess the truths of the hidden provocations in such words. It is complicated stress and duress which elicits such words.

Unfortunately, it is seldom pointedly shown that the *real* victims in such words are the children. A climate of total lack of feeling for the feelings of the children is the rule, rather than the exception, in divorce. While the legal machinery of the law lumberingly arrives at the ultimate divorce, the children have no spokesman, no impartial defender, no words for their grief at the absence of a beloved parent. Does anyone analyze the total lack of concern for them that such a remark reveals? They are no more than helpless pawns by which such mothers gain ends that are fully to their own advantage, while at the same time they cleverly draw sympathy to themselves by the direct or tacitly understood remarks, "Yes, he's foot-loose and fancy-free while I'm stuck with the children." Meanwhile, there is an objective truth in this mother's wish that her children shall not see their father. Regardless of the provocation by her husband, such mothers show no compassion, no empathy towards their own children. Imprisoned in their own anger, they cannot, apparently, consider what divisions of this kind can do to the hearts of little ones.

Does the final divorce end these win-lose tactics? By no means. There is no law to legislate the screams, the insults, the devious character assassination that creates the "drop-out father." If a woman can provoke a man to a violent act, what then? Every subsequent court appearance costs money. Mr. Average Citizen finally retreats. Visitation days become an agonizing ordeal for everyone; the subtle changes of invisible child abuse causes the thoughtful parent to reason, "Perhaps they will be better off without my visits."

Aggression in young girls and women has never been sufficiently examined. In both sexes it is frequently of sexual origin, and it may well be that in divorce it comprises a substitute orgasm. There is a deep conspiracy of silence among men concerning the violent "little woman." With reference to a broken arm, the six-foot husband of a minus-five-foot, ninety-eight-pound woman said, "Who would believe me?" And, when asked, "How?" replied, "A man has to protect his head from a wrought iron plant stand!" Ironically, the pathetic little mother in this instance accuses her husband of the very acts she herself has committed and boasted of committing. Has any lawyer brought up the matter of projection in which the aggressive woman endows her mate with the very violence which lies within herself? In this case, not one.

An even stranger phenomenon in our divorce structure is the fact that the woman need not endure the vacuum of personal involvement that must be endured by a man. Her round of personal tasks, in one form or another, goes on. The man, in this case, took his clothes out of the garbage can, endured the changing of locks on premises purchased with his own sweat, and took up the amputated life that remained to him. Somehow he must learn to accept society's stereotyped judgment of the "abusive male." It may take years before these same arbiters of law (social workers, police officers, lawyers, politicians and family court judges) see *more* than the tip of the marital iceberg. When the female goes on to "invite" abuse from another husband, or, worse, transfer her temper and hostilities to her growing children, time, and the law's protection at the time of crisis, will have placed her beyond the reach of law.

Feeling totally free of blame, there are several strategies used by women to evade guilt feelings for their own actions. These will range from such excuses as "He did it first," as if the action of a mate provides a cause for their own behavior, or, because she would feel guilty for her own actions, she must find something for which to blame her husband. Another strategy is the argument, "He had it coming to him." To maintain that he "deserves" what he gets lessens her own potential guilt feeling. The strategy of depreciation is another device, since this helps them to justify the "logic" of their own actions, which is usually summarized by saying, "He's no good anyway. What right has he to complain?" Apparently they feel no tie to any moral code if they can prove to their own satisfaction that "he" has it coming. Or, if she can prove that "he" is against her, she will interpret almost any situation as "unfair."

But the "best" strategy is to hang onto the encouragement gained from the movies and television. These offer marital

41

stereotypes on which to fasten their own marital fantasies. What begins as an innocent evening of watching television is, for the sick marriage partner, a vehicle for transferring fantasy to real life, so that they move from the "soap opera" to literal action.

Similarly, if women have no feeling for the feelings of their little children, if the small sigh, the look of delight, the wave of baby hands, the clutch of little fingers arouses no tender feelings, their "lawlessness" transgresses the unwritten law, and we had better begin to take the lack of "natural" feeling with much more seriousness than we have shown to date.

10

Divorce: Without the Consent of the Governed

*Children are sent for another purpose
than merely to keep up the race . . .
to enlarge our hearts; and to make us
unselfish and full of kindly sympathies
and affections; to give our souls higher aims;
to call out all our faculties to extended
enterprise and exertion; and to bring round
our fireside bright faces, happy smiles,
and loving, tender hearts. My soul
blesses the great Father every day, that
he has gladdened the earth with children. (M. Howitt)*

A Case History of Jack and Jill

Dear F.B.I.

Would you please try to find my daddy? I am twelve years old, and I have a new daddy. But I remember my *real* daddy and I would just like to see him again. My sister is two years older than I am, and she says I'm silly to write to you, but I do not dare to ask my mother because I can remember how she would scream, "Get out!" whenever my daddy tried to come home. Yours truly, Jackie Jones.

And by the deceptively simple device of screaming, "Get out!" a woman may, to her own satisfaction, find herself in possession of a house earned by her husband's money. Never mind the terrible truths that must exist for such a wife and such a husband; two basic human instincts are dramatically illustrated. The diminutive mother's scream did not occur without provocation. Human "fight or flight" reactions are clear. SHE fights; HE flies. He cannot bear to be seen by his children as such a man, but who can fully explore the feelings of the children? Since I was such a child, I wish to speak for those who cannot speak for themselves.

Did that father leave his home and children after the first series of screams, "Get out! Get out!" No, there are sordid details in the death-struggle of any marriage that need no replay. Bitterly the wife says she never wants the children to see their father again. It is not difficult to accomplish. Her parents will give her emotional, even financial support; her friends listen and pity. Whatever his status, the husband often wants his children to have a "home." Visiting privileges are granted. Do the parents *see* their children's divided, bewildered, conflicting, vacillating, torn, emotional attachments? It is usually the father, conditioned by the harsh realities of the workaday world, who decides they will be better off not faced with such conflicts.

Where does this leave a two-year-old boy and a four-year-old sister at their parents' divorce? It was evident to any number of observers that the children adored both parents. However, the close observer could see a preoccupied, brooding look on the little mother's face at the ecstatic cries from Jill of, "Daddy, daddy!" whenever her father appeared. Later events proved that the not-pleased look on Jill's mother's face could be read as, "Ha! I've had them all day; I'm cooped up with them; I cook and clean and scrub and *he* gets all the glory!"

Jealousy is a common parental occurrence. Nearly everyone has heard playful remarks by fathers and mothers to their children, "Whom do you love the most, mommy or daddy?"

Perhaps it is only the adult who remembers himself so questioned who refrains from asking it of his own children. In the case of Jill and Jack, when little brother was born, it was evident that he too "came alive" when his daddy was around. But what is more natural? A fact apparently ignored by the advocates of unisex is that *maleness* has a more profound function than the impregnation with sperm. Fatherhood is needed by all of us, male and female alike, just as is motherhood. If mothers could be taught that they lose no love, and are in no way threatened when their children are enthusiastic over daddy, the cradle-rocking hand could do much toward promoting universal peace. Conversely, the same is true of the fathers who undercut their wives.

Unfortunately, after adults have recovered their equilibrium following a marital explosion, very young children do not so recover. According to Erik H. Erikson in *Childhood and Society,* their earliest remembrances and sensations of recollected comfort from either parent *is never erased.* Experience, for the very young, must contain a continuous "predictability," since a life-long establishment of mistrust is set up when the presence of either parent is permanently withdrawn. The full-grown person brings with him forever, the infantile "patterning" of his parents. An inner craving which cannot be articulated by the child is implanted.

This inner craving for what is denied (in this case, the comforting parent) is followed by a pervasive doubt and sense of badness (never analyzed by the child); the sense of badness grows when parents use the very young as ploys in their mutual power plays. In Jackie at age two, a marked aggression and defiance became evident. Jill became an accomplished actress. Indeed, the mother lived out her own fantasies by promoting the child as a model, yet in the life of her feelings, Jill learned secrecy and manipulation. Unable to endure the derogatory remarks about her adored father, a self-conscious desire to placate and please her mother could be seen in this perceptive child's attempt to maintain a precarious hold on security and comfort from the only source left to her.

It must never be thought that I am advocating an artificial

prolonging of the marital ties "for the sake of the children." I am not. This places a burden on children that does more harm than divorce. I am urging adults, no matter how angry and hurt they are, to guard their children from imbibing their parents' bitterness. This can only be done by realizing the child's proclivity to *love* and his child's-eye view of parents as the objects of his love. I did not "see" what my mother saw in my father; I only knew deep, deep within the marrow of my bones that I loved him.

11

Christmas: Divorce Reform

AN OPEN LETTER TO WIVES

*Give sorrow words: the grief that does not speak
whispers the o'er-fraught heart, and bids it break.
(Macbeth IV: Shakespeare)*

"And in today, tomorrow walks." If there is one gift an older woman can give to a younger woman, it is the assurance of Coleridge's words in this maxim. But it is a truth that can be both assuring and frightening.

You are a divorced woman and you have custody of your children. In this development, you have been honored. Most frequently a male judge has tacitly agreed with the old cliche, "The hand that rocks the cradle rules the world." It is ordinarily not difficult to decide that you are better equipped to care for your children than any woman your ex-husband can hire, or any woman he might choose as your successor. All the solemn rights of blood are yours. Here it is interesting to note that among all the arguments raised for women's rights, very few voices are heard expanding on the rights we always had, our "cradle rule."

Those who adhere to the principles of "patterning" and "conditioning" will tell us that wishes, dreams, hopes, feelings and associations are directly related to what we, like other organisms, were taught to "expect." It is not necessary to examine the ramifications of these psychological viewpoints since we have an excellent analogy in nature. Incontrovertible proof surrounds us. We plant a rose; we raise a rose; we plant a grain of corn; we reap an ear of corn. In each and every planting results are contingent upon the "soil" in which each is planted. Variables in soil and weather conditions may give us a blighted rose or no more than a few abortive leaves. In the kernel of corn, we may likewise harvest an ear with too many gaps to be edible.

Less graphic and less acceptable is the idea that the same "law" operates with regard to our mental and emotional states. In our "cradle rule" we "plant" expectations in our children. A painful memory may never be verbalized, but given the right set of circumstances, i.e. "soil," that painful memory will grow to be an exact duplicate of what was planted.

At the Christmas season, thousands of remembrances emerge. As a divorced wife, you will decorate your tree with or without the help of family or friends. In any event, it will *all* be different. Unless you are very well in command of your emotions, "he" will not be there. But "he" is not the person he may actually be in the eyes of your children. Especially is this true of preschool children's parental images. You two *are* their universe! A pre-Christmas session in emotional detachment with love should be made a mandatory law for all divorced parents of preschool children. Why? Because the preschooler's involuntary, "Will daddy be here?" cries out to be answered, "Yes, daddy will be here." The unlearned and ignorant will retort, "They have short memories. They don't even miss him!" Whereas the memory of the zero to five-year-old merely goes underground. The seed has been planted and will yield its inevitable harvest. Nevertheless, the expectation that both

48

parents will be there deserves more notice than Santa Claus!

As a divorced or separated wife, if you have read thus far, you will attempt to ease yourself from granting your child's silent or verbalized wish. A thick volume of rationales can be logically summoned. You will try to account for your refusal by recalling all your former husband's faults. Worse, you will compensate for your own faults and failings by exaggerating his. This will go beyond all bounds if your own self-hatred is too deep or too powerful for you to see it or face it with your conscious mind. You will minimize your own marital failures and reward yourself for doing so by passing your own guilts on to him. However, refusal by either mate on the above grounds carries the same conclusion.

Both of you should know that one of the most pleasant things you can do for another human is to show him that he is needed. If you, as a wife, can shelve your resentment in this season of good will you may harvest a crop of chain reactions that will effect your child's life-long expectations.

To explain: You cannot postpone either your child's living or your own. You live today! Payment plans do not extend to the living of our lives. We cannot promise ourselves that tomorrow will be different. As Pascal says, we cannot simply be "hoping to live, and looking forward always to being happy." *Now* is all we possess. This Christmas! And it is this Christmas that you can both live and be happy not "because of," but "in spite of." However, if you cannot set your mental attitude for this present minute, nothing *external*—be that money, love or gifts—can grant it to you.

The only cure lies in seeing yourself as a person who can *act* and not merely *react*. Until you can do this, you are not even a mother but a puppet of your divorce, a puppet for whom what "he" has said or done, or some event or circumstances, dictates how you will feel and react. In short, you are a slave, not to your broken marriage, but to any outward circumstance. Yes, you may have to give up some of your cherished resentments, but what is that if you can look back and know that *you* put the magic in that little face and voice which carols, "Daddy was here!"

Unless you have joined that too common chorus, "If I have my way, he'll never see these children!" Then your tomorrows will harvest your resolve. All the unhappiness you inflict upon another will come back into your own life. It does not matter what "he" has done, short of murder or child abuse, the nurture of our children lies biologically on *us*. If we play "god" with the affections of a little child we are flaunting the unwritten law of the universe itself. Whatever is planted in the "soil" of a human life grows in terrible resemblance to the seeds planted, whether such seed is visible or invisible. "Though hand joined in hand [we] shall not go unpunished." To deny this is to deny the large print of the universe.

12

The "Soul" of Furniture

*For so it falls out
that what we have we prize not to the worth
Whiles we enjoy it, but being lack'd and lost,
Why, then we rack the value, then we find
The virtue that possession would not show us
Whiles it was ours.
(Much Ado About Nothing III: Shakespeare)*

There was nothing the dying millionaire could not buy, yet he was constantly asking for something his attendants could not supply. They bent closely to hear the mumbled words, and went out quickly to purchase the requested roses. They had known he was fond of beauty. He had spent several fortunes purchasing Europe's treasures from its impoverished aristocracy. Perhaps more had been spent in his lavish gardens, but this they would have no way of knowing.

When the roses came, the old man's agitation grew worse. However, along with his agitation, his words became more audible. "Rosebud! Rosebud!" They took away the roses and brought a single rose. Again, his agitation became so intense that at length he died.

After his death, impersonal employees sorted the old man's possessions, burning much that obviously dated from the days of his poverty. When a warehouse attendant asked the supervisor about a battered sled, he was told, "Burn it!"

Musingly, the warehouse boy looked down at the weathered lettering and commented succinctly, "Rosebud is sure a strange name for a sled."

But much more than a senile nostalgia is contained in this anecdote from the life of William Randolph Hearst. The enduring nature of love for childhood's possessions and associations could be told and retold if people with enough concern would care to trace them.

In similar fashion, an alert little lady of ninety-two in a cluttered room of an old people's home has a huge, soiled American flag leaning against one corner. Even in a littered room it appears a grotesque intrusion. Why is it there? She mourns the things "they" would not let her take along. With charming ingenuity she serves her guests the traditional coffee and cake so dear to her heart by opening a dresser drawer. Upon the opened drawer, she places a large tray and a lace tablecloth which covers the remaining part of the dresser. Her best blue china cups are tremblingly displayed, and cake appears from its perennial place on top of the radiator. Invariably she prefaces her hospitality by saying, "I wish I could serve you a turkey dinner the way I used to do."

To those who know her, she retains her sense of identity and usefulness in being a hostess. In her mind, the dresser drawer becomes a later version of her large dining room table. The treasured cups hold back for a brief while the inexorable sweep of the years. And the flag? She is engaged in a dialogue with herself each morning as she lifts her eyes from her bed to the opposite corner where it stands. Will she ever get enough courage to tell "them" her wishes regarding that flag? She wants it on her coffin, then folded and placed beside her heart before her burial. It is all that is tangible from the son she gave for an adopted country she loves with a fierce patriotism.

Do children care? They are not consulted when mother, in her concern for a "picture-book" house, throws away a battered childhood treasure. They may protest, "But mom, I wanted to keep that!" They are told in no-nonsense tones, "You're not keeping that smelly old junk!"

After divorce the attachment to what is familiar is an emotional necessity. For the preschooler, divorce is an overwhelmingly strange amputation for which he has no words. One half of his universe has been taken away. The sudden absence, the change in attitudes on the part of surrounding adults, the intense fear of abandonment, and the distress of the once married pair has blocked his own potential for parenting. Rarely do the embittered pair recognize the nonverbal anguish of their young children. In attempting to divide household possessions, little thought is given to the child's attachment for items which adults may not give a second glance.

To dad, that breakfront is visible proof of his ability to provide for his family, simultaneously an ego-booster and an inner satisfaction, and deeply related to self-sufficiency. To mom, it represents a wish that may date from her little-girl days. "At last I have just what Aunt Mabel had!" Or, it may simply be the concrete evidence of a joint love for the beautiful. The treasures it holds are more than objects. That pitcher was purchased on a drive up to the country. The contentment of that day is fused with its blue luster. His mother gave her that antique candy jar (and she can jolly well have it back, the horrid old hag!). But to the little ones the removal of such pieces is linked to a need for a predictable world.

Dividing their furnishings, the couple attach no importance to the children's feelings. When a grandmother received the old trunk she had once given to her daughter-in-law, she too, gave no thought to the preschooler. On a visiting day, the withdrawn little one shouted spontaneously in tones of surprised recognition, "Mommy's trunk! Mommy's trunk!" That day, the children (both preschoolers) threw themselves into frenetic activity as if to ease some new pain through shouting and jumping and thumping grandma's furniture. The "soul" of possessions are in their associations. That chain from a mother's own hair, made for her husband's watch, remains forever, "a bracelet of bright hair about the bone."

> That instant's flash
> In which a little thing
> Is loved,
> Wraps it in immortality,
> At sight of which
> A kindred eye is kindled.
> Nor knows that answering spark
> Why common things
> Are not dumb stones,
> But have a voice invisible
> Echoing soundlessly
> From that far distant breath of love,
> All briefly and imperfectly bestowed.

In our throw-away culture, we give too little heed to the love of children for "things" that take on a dimension of "soul" because they belonged to that precious place a child calls "home."

13

The Travesty of the Shared Holiday

As the presence of those we love
is as a double life,
so absence,
in its anxious longings,
in its sense of vacancy,
is a foretaste of death. (Jameson)

It was the first time the children were dressed in their holiday best. Even at ages four and five, the consciousness of something special was evident. They walked with the proud dignity of miniature adults. There was none of the usual bounding up the stairs with hands on the step above; this time, each took a firm hold on the banister and ascended sedately conscious of their stiff new shoes and crisp, unwrinkled clothes. Even our welcoming hugs took on a formality and deliberation unlike the spontaneous hugs of the ordinary visit.

I held each one at arm's length, sensing their need to be admired; to give recognition to the "specialness" of their clothes in tacit honor of the day. How proud they were! Indeed, it was the first time in two years of weekly visits that they were sent in their holiday best. Not even at Christmas had they been sent in anything but shabby attire and worn sneakers—not because I had not given them clothes (I had), but in subtle scorn for their daddy's people.

After giving them many outfits which I never again saw them wear, I was left with the expedient of keeping several sets of clothes for them here, in preparation for their brief Sunday visits. But what child wants to *leave* a new outfit? And, as a one-time mother, now a grandmother, I would never burden that love-hungry child with any question which would put a loved mother in a questionable position. A strange reticence fell over Janey's face when I asked if she would like to keep her new dress in "her room." It was actually my office, but from the day of her first visit, she had exclaimed in happy, possessive tones, "My little room! My *very own* little room!" It followed that she later brought toys to leave there. And every small towel in the bathroom became a Janey-towel until little brother began claiming an equal number which he chose to call *his* "boy-towels." Later they would happily take a towel in their pockets with a plaintive, "But grandma, can't I take it home?"—pathetic little efforts to unite their divided lives.

But their divided little hearts have had the legal assistance of four lawyers for the embattled parents, as well as a judge. A system of alternating holidays was looked upon as one of the more "fair" aspects of the divorce. Accordingly, a father may see his children seven hours once a week and on alternate holidays between the hours of noon and 7:00 P.M. On each holiday designated "X", the husband shall have visitation during the year 19--, and each even numbered year thereafter. On each holiday designated "A", the husband shall have visitation during the odd numbered years thereafter.

The list reads:
1. New Year's Day
2. Christmas
3. Thanksgiving

4. Labor Day
5. July 4th
6. Memorial Day
7. Easter
8. Lincoln's Birthday
9. Washington's Birthday
10. Mother's Day—Father's Day

If we include the parents, this is a team of seven adults who fail to ask with regard to the above list: *To whom is this fair?* No one hears the chorus of children who cry, "Why can't we be together?" The horrible irony of most couple's efforts to arrive at amicable visiting rights is the fact that the children have, literally, no vote or even representation in the matter.

In the case of Janey and her brother, holidays would find their mother preparing to invite all the little cousins from "her" side of the family. It was easy to surmise the happy preparations in which the children shared. Why? Clearly, the mother had no concern for the torn loyalties with which these little ones accompanied their father. Should the father have denied himself that holiday's visiting rights? Seeing their longing to remain with their cousins, he volunteered, saying, "Would you rather stay home?" The "tie" to daddy, that not even death can break, asserted itself. With a backward look at "home" in its festive holiday preparations, they left to accompany daddy to the "other" grandparents' home.

Janey entered valiantly into the preparations in her paternal grandmother's kitchen. Donning a pretty apron, she "helped" with the family feast at which no little cousins would be present. Little brother, unable to take on such a double role, crawled into his father's lap and asked plaintively, "Can't I go home to mommy's party?" With an aching heart, grandma (on daddy's side) hurried her flurried dinner and said, "Do take them home, so they can share the day with their little cousins too."

The little ones, usually such happy little gourmets, were unable to eat the pushed-ahead dinner. For the adults who sensed the children's divided hearts, it was painful to watch or to ignore. Holiday meals which are intended to reinforce family ties become a mockery. Indeed, perhaps it will require a world famine before we realize that *any* meal is more than a meal. For the most insensitive, the family table is a sharing that far transcends the common elements of which it is composed.

What of those children whose mothers remarry? What of mothers who succeed in giving their children as father-substitutes men who are perhaps superior in all ways to the children's fathers? What of the kindly, understanding, sensitive, calm, predictable men who restore a measure of equilibrium to homes, while the "real fathers" drop out?

Jane and Joan, whose mother remarried when Joan, the younger, was twelve years old, recall the envy that was theirs at picnics in the park. When neighbors and friends gathered for potluck meals and other children would say spontaneously, "Gee, but I like your dad!" why did Jane and Joan always respond so coldly? Why would they go out of their way to say, "He's not our *real* father!" Why did they almost resent their step-father's genuine decency? A deep sense of injury and loss remains in such children. Why did each girl marry men who were *not* like their step-father, but men very much like the father they had not seen since their preschool days? Even without exhaustive studies it is clear that divorce can never erase the organism's tie to the missing parent.

What about the high school senior whose parents felt that at last they could drop all pretense and get their divorce? After all, Jack would be entering college in the fall. A teacher who had had Jack as a freshman and later as a senior noted the drastic change in his attitude. When she learned of his parents' impending divorce, she understood. A brilliant student, his grades betrayed no change. The conflict was kept repressed except for a strange cynicism that often aligned his classmates against him.

At Christmas, unable to endure a disunited home, he took his bicycle and headed for a warmer climate, seeking from nature the "warmth" that home no longer held. He was killed by a passing motorist. No one would dream of attributing the accident to his inability to bear the "shared" segments of a "his" and "hers" holiday.

14

Disposable Fathers

Parents wonder why the streams are bitter,
when they themselves have poisoned the fountain.
(Locke)

"But he sets such a bad example for the children!" says Jane, when the counselor urges her to accept joint custody in her divorce action. Of course, custody reinforces the "best interests" rule, but it also gives to embittered women a power of judgment that *neither* embattled parent should have. Usually (in 98 percent of the cases), it is decided that if the mother proves her own "fitness" she is, traditionally, given custody. And hardly a day's newspaper appears without reporting some "incident" of child abduction by either father or mother. Yet for every such report, you have dozens of unreported cases where visitation is denied to the defendant, whether that be father or mother. Very rarely do these denials reach family court, since the vast majority of divorcing couples cannot afford the legal fees.

Where money differences, infidelity, gambling or drinking have been the "arena" for marital fights, divorce has given each battle-hardened spouse a far more potent "weapon" than marital differences could ever pose. Paradoxically, that lethal and helpless "weapon" is the child. In the struggle for one-parent survival, anger gives a better impetus and drive to one's determination than being submissive or even agreeable. Separation has removed the need to react to what was once regarded as the "cause" for divorce. Indignation must now find a new target. What better way to hurt the "other" than through the children? And too often indignation burns so hotly the children are forgotten. The parent who denies the other his visitation rights is convinced that the children would be better off if they never saw the offending father or mother.

Judges try to consider the complicated needs of children, but the odious comparisons which juxtapose "best interests" and "better parent" should be entirely eliminated from the proceedings. A nondiscriminatory law should be enacted whereby battling adults are legally prevented from decision-making which affects their children. Mandatory counseling and a legal time-lapse would be the appointed co-agents to provide for a measure of calm and detachment to develop. Nor should children *ever* bear the burden of having to choose!

Where children choose, decisions are based on the most flimsy and fluctuating foundations. Often it may be based on which parent administered the most recent restriction or which parent cared enough to correct his child, in which case the character-building discipline is held against that parent. The criticism, "Mom's too busy to listen to us," may be related to her valiant attempt to hold down a full-time job, to keep house, cook, clean, shop and be all things to family, home and profession. Such women often raise self-sufficient children, but at great cost to themselves which, at the stage of a marital break-up, turns their very efficiency against them.

On the other hand, a child may choose the father because, in the separation that precedes divorce, visits with dad take on an aura of specialness that gives his visitation rights a Santa Claus glow. A totally artificial relationship is encouraged in such arrangements. The very brevity and "company-manners" rarity denies the father all ordinary or routine rights of fathering. Worse, it encourages children to "play" one parent against the other. Meanwhile, the mother's "boyfriend" may become the ninety hours a week presence in the home, hardly an "equitable" division of parenting in the eyes of a *real* father.

It should be evident to all judges that if one parent wants the other denied all visitation, it does not necessarily follow that the "defendant" (father or mother) is bad for the child. And what happens to even one child speaks for all children! Precisely because it is so easy to "color" the viewpoints of children, it is an all too common practice on the part of divorcing parents to demean the absent parent. It gives a young mother a measure of relief for her own guilt in the break-up of a marriage to say to her children, "Your father doesn't want to see you today!" "Your father prefers the bar!" "Your father prefers his whore!" (These are documented quotes!) But even where a mother uses the utmost tact and refinement, and says merely, "Your father is away on business," the mother's mood transmits itself.

The hidden drama which such remarks evoke in the heart of a child has not been sufficiently explored. Upon hearing such remarks, most preschool and early elementary age children remain inarticulate. A toy will suddenly absorb all interest. Subtle changes will take place in the child which the mood-driven parent does not notice. The child may shout, "Ouch!" and pretend he has stubbed his toe. He may even feign illness. He may become unaccountably fearful, or aggressive, or withdrawn and quiet. Again, he may grow restless and irritable. Never will he protest or defend the maligned parent. The real response of the very young child must be studied in another context. The conflict of his parents will be re-enacted in his dreams and in his play. This will be a nonverbalized struggle from which there is seldom any escape! If words could be granted to such children, they would perhaps be:

I'm afraid!

I *must* have been a bad boy!

I *must* have been a bad girl!

When such children grow up they may be intellectually enlightened by a psychiatrist who assures them that the lifelong burden of guilt goes back to their parents' divorce, but such intellectual recognition merely renders the guilt comprehensible. As adults, these children can recognize the causes of their guilt mentally, but their feelings and emotions require constant reassurances that they are not "bad."

Do parents understand that to a child *they* have all power? That the "Our Father which art in heaven" is really not a far-away God, but the embodiment of a daddy who can be seen and trusted? How puzzling, how inexplicable that a mother and father who were the source of all that spelled comfort and security are now part of a world gone wrong! A child can only reason, "Mommy and daddy *can't* be wrong! They are big! They are strong!" And so deep is the *need* to cling to parental *rightness* that the sense of helplessness is turned upon the self. "I *must* have been bad," reasons the child subconsciously.

Pulled and divided as they are between father and mother, children will, in their longings for togetherness, exaggerate the virtues of a missing parent. To compensate for unbearable absence, a child may fantasize and endow the other parent with all manner of personal preferences and projections. Grown to adulthood, such children become manipulative experts, and alternate between realistic character appraisals of those they love, and wishful fantasy. They are often unable to maintain a wholehearted relationship with anyone because they themselves have been made into a kind of human "negotiable currency" between their battling parents, in their most impressionable and formative years.

Life situations which demand a certain wholeness are met with doubleminded uncertainties and insecurity; relationships which call for the undivided heart are entered upon with serious doubts of self-worth. Whichever parent manages to impute the most guilt to the other leaves a residue of guilt in the child-grown-up which inwardly asks, "Am I like him?" or, "Am I like her?" Such ego disturbances are not always evident in obvious neurotic symptoms, but they persist with a loss of wholeness which is constantly being updated as life-relationships expand.

A revision of the entire historical argument with regard to custody is long overdue. Where tradition upholds the mother's nurturing relationship with the child, the child's need for the father has not been adequately explored. Children can no longer be relegated to a "poker chip" status between their parents and their parents' lawyers.

Clearly, where children are concerned, and where their lives are to be divided and segmented, men's rights, women's rights and equal rights are not the issues. Any child is animated by the same spirit as his father and mother. Environment may modify, but it never eradicates the innate personality. With regard to this truth, a prosthesis and a surrogate parent are similar. We may compliment an amputee for his dexterity in the use of a prosthetic arm or leg, but even the best-adjusted amputee would rather be whole again.

Similarly, divorce is amputation for children, and far different from being orphaned. The notion of source, origin, roots are all contained in fatherhood. A father is both author and creator. Much more than a mere sex act is involved. A father is the first person in the chain of the begetting process. The sanctity of this distinction should give us a glimpse into the eternal oneness and mystique of parenthood.

Unfortunately, humans will take their life-directions from any source that pleases them. The more immediate the gratification, the better, even though history and religion teach us that the ability to delay personal gratification is the mark of highest intelligence and wisdom. Perhaps we would not now be so plagued with the raucous wordiness of the equal rights movement if men had not abdicated their historical position of leadership. Or did some male editor, with bleak humor, decide that women's claims of repression and discrimination would "sell"? Sadly, it offers no refuge to children who are being "traded" indiscriminately for wall-to-wall carpets, gadgets ad infinitum, travel, and a spurious freedom which is no freedom at all.

A labyrinth of complicated causes may be summoned to elaborate on our modern decadence, but the alarming rise in divorces is contributing to the emergence of a generation of emotional cripples. Children from broken homes are riddled with fears and hostility and hatred. As teenagers, their only defenses are a pervasive cynicism and anger which is transferred to almost any authority figure: parents, teachers, policemen, superiors, government. Tragically, the chain reactions of parental immaturity, which lie at the heart of any divorce, render parents blind to the needs of their children.

Divorcing parents seem to survive best by summoning a real or imagined indignation against their mates, and from this they draw a perverse energy. This is their strongest motivation when they use their children as the pawns in their macabre power-play of marital chess. But while they are doing this they are also teaching these little ones that, along with disposable tissues, towels, paper plates, cups, utensils, they also have disposable parents.

We face a dragon-seed future—Cadmus updated! To teach the human heart that what it instinctively loves is disposable, is to shape a future in which such children, so taught, will move beyond our present decadence. Where *we* have begun with the fetus in our attempts to legalize abortions, *they* may eliminate the old-age homes. It is not inconceivable that the disregard with which such children were handled will reap a harvest of disregard for old age. Will today's forgotten children one day erect life-exit chambers to a generation which taught them that fathers were disposable?

15

To Have or Not to Have Children

To will what God wills
is the only science that gives us rest.
(Longfellow)

Wives are often shocked that their husbands do not respond as they themselves do to the children they have jointly begotten. Since women literally carry the oneness of the child-begetting act for three-quarters of a year, the growing fetus leads them into thoughts they had never expected to have. This is true whether they are contemplating an abortion, or happily anticipating a child. It is evidence of a widely applicable truth from an ancient book, "A little child shall lead them" (Isa. 11:6). Very often we women are offended that our husbands do not share this day-by-day sense of threeness that is now ours.

A sense of aloneness, despite a kindly mate, often makes itself felt. Perhaps this is one of the many reasons that husbands are now permitted to be present at the entire travail of birth. It cannot be other than true that if a husband is a busy, hard-working man, he may give little or no evidence of solicitous concern for his wife's "delicate condition." It is, after all, a thoroughly natural development. But the need to be kind to herself gives the wife *time* to store up and ponder all manner of imagined slights and grievances. A common resentment was voiced by a wife who had tried for years to become pregnant. "Once he reaches his orgasm it's all over for him!" And she patted her protruding middle.

Of course it is not "all over" for the man. There are men who feel more snared by the prospect of parenthood than women. Sensing this, one woman said with deep concern, "Do you feel trapped, dear?" Yet this same woman gave her life for the child she had willingly "risked" having. I refer to Catherine in *A Farewell To Arms.* To some readers this seems a distinct reversal of roles. The emotional and economic responsibility traditionally the male's can never be the "trap" that the enveloping and growing body of the female becomes. To digress briefly, the word "trap" places the entire child bearing process in a negative context, and it is the modern view of sex which contributes to the idea of a biological snare. Yet for husbands as well as wives, the advent of a child brings about divergent and wholly complementary roles.

Abortion and planned parenthood suggest that sex should be entered upon with no aftermath except a sense of well-being or orgasmic release. In effect, sex is modern man's "therapy." Manuals and "how-to" books, ad nauseum, have subdivided our bodies into such mechanized terms as zones with longitudes and latitudes and polarities soon to follow. The implications are that by pressing this or that "zone" you will get this or that response. Discovery, surprise, and personal exploration, and spiritual union are left to old-fashioned religionists. Are these marriage manuals true? Extremely true. When a husband, after reading *The Hite Report,* tells his wife, "I know all about you," he is not far from wrong, if by "all" he means sexual response. Most thinking women prefer the ancient allusion which was said far more succintly, if more abstractly, ". . . I am fearfully and wonderfully made" (Ps. 139:14). Or, "My beloved is a garden of spices." Can we ever regain the mystery of sex that only lovers knew?

In an age preoccupied with physical beauty, the wife's mirror-image of her distended middle contributes to her sense of aloneness. It does not help that self-image much to pick up mass-media's recent emphasis, "Is your husband younger looking than you are?" In the childbearing equation a kindly mate can make this a period in which the *inner* person becomes the wife's real self-image. What was attractive and loved in the physical is now transferred in subtle ways to the self *behind* the once attractive exterior.

Truly, on its most ennobling level, sex is "life's longing for itself." Persons who enter into sex with a conscious or unconscious view to pure pleasure will always be doomed to *ultimate* disappointment. No, not at first, because God does indeed wrap His most solemn processes in joy, but never does sex reach its zenith until the thought of another life's begetting becomes a part of the act. The entire mystique is not understood beforehand, but in reflection and analysis *after*, perhaps long after, the act when "the hey-dey in the blood is tame . . . and waits upon the judgment." Thus the body becomes a holy vessel bearing God's inheritance, since a believer cannot be anything but deeply convinced that "Children *are* an inheritance from the Lord."

Again, we live in an age which looks first to economics. A poverty-stricken mother found herself, in spite of contraceptives, pregnant for the fourth time. Searching the Scriptures for comfort and reassurance, she was brought to a happy acceptance and rest in her "predicament." Against all common sense, she claimed the promise, ". . . my God shall supply all your need," *not* according to your need but "according to his riches . . ." (Phil. 4:19). From that "leap of faith" she rested in an all-sufficient God.

No abracadabra magic followed. Her husband did not suddenly receive a raise. Were circumstances markedly changed? No, nothing changed outwardly except her growing fetus. All of her child's needs were provided by the "charity" of friends. Were she to have shopped for her baby she would have chosen far more simply than the abundance with which she was "showered." Jokingly, her family said of her new arrival, "He's certainly not much for looks!" She did not reply, but an odd sentence echoed in her mind, "The stone which the builders rejected, the same is become the head of the corner" (Matt. 21:42). Years later *that* child became a man of God who was trusted with unusual honors in this present age. She will not betray either her own name or that of her son, but the truth of her experience should be recorded as an antidote for young mothers who reject the pill, and find failure in contraceptives. Children *are* an inheritance from God; it is a word that has not and cannot fail!

Another word should be added to it, "And God shall choose our inheritance for us." This is an on-going process in *every* area of the life of the believer. Moreover, to believe this in the face of unfavorable circumstances lends a radiance to the most humdrum life.

It may be argued that such a belief relieves the individual of the responsibility for choice and self-directedness, but to believe is an act of will and a far higher *inner-directness* than that which sets self as the "captain of fate." Indeed, to choose such a truth becomes the highest and most difficult of choices.

Why is such an acquiescence so difficult? Because, if we know ourselves at all, we will admit that one of our deepest inclinations is the will to want our own way! Given no restraints, we would "turn, everyone to his own way." However, in the matter of child bearing we are faced with overwhelmingly urgent evidence of over-population, world-hunger, and ecological warnings that the world food-chain is not equal to our growing needs. *Shall we measure those needs as they are now being measured?* No, for the believer, the expectation must, where children are concerned, be the "foolish" expectation of miraculous supply. We must expect to receive *unexplored* responses to our needs.

It is not easy to appear a "fool" in the eyes of the world's finest minds, or even in the secret recesses of our own intelligence. Such belief is not rational; it is suprarational. We must believe (in *any* context) God's promise, "Behold I will do a *new* thing!" To people who have tested this in the most pragmatic circumstances, God *has* done new things in the past; His mercies are *new* every morning of the present; and *He will continue* to surprise us with new discoveries in the future. In no area of life is this *sure* word more true than where child bearing and the life-force unite.

16

Internal Divorce:
("For the Sake of the Children")

There is no right
without a parallel duty,
. . . no greatness
without self-denial. (Liebar)

How contradictory it seems for a judge in pronouncing his decision before a divorcing couple to grant custody to the mother. This is done in 98 percent of the cases with the qualifying phrase, ". . . for the sake of the children." What is the contradiction? The implication that, of the two, the wife is *less* wrong. Among all the wrongs that led to their divorce, all such custody arrangements imply a double standard of justice. It goes without saying that a great deal more than guilt or innocence enters the judge's decision. "For the sake of the children" encompasses a wide range of reasons, from economics to our traditional understanding of maternalism.

While a judge may use the phrase, "for the sake of the children" with impunity, a married couple using the same words as a rationale for remaining married are regarded as some sort of masochistic freaks. For the married, the term is anathema! A library of child-guidance facts and figures would accuse such couples of placing intolerable burdens on their children. Indeed, it is well known that *any* difficulty which leads a couple to the question of divorce will be absorbed by the children, if not directly, by osmosis.

It follows that if the welfare of the children decrees custody to the mother, this is a vote in favor of the mother, and not necessarily in the best interests of the children. Lost sight of is the fact that any couple deciding to stay married "for the sake of the children," are committing themselves to a "vote" in favor of their offspring. Their very *lives* are stating that as their children did not "ask" to be born, they, as adults, that is, as parents, are less vulnerable to meeting the problems of life than are their unformed children. Implicit in such a decision is the recognition that children "see" their parents with a love that springs from an entirely different perspective than that which is seen from the viewpoints of two quarreling adults.

Before their marital problems led to divorce, the same couple lovingly, happily, eagerly accepted their new life roles of being and doing for the sake of a yet-to-be-born child. And for all couples, whether married, divorced, or divorcing, two ancient and tested precepts can become an anchor as well as a beacon for behavior. The precepts are simple, but not simplistic, and they are far from easy to follow: "Children are an inheritance from God." (For the truth of this adage, do not go to the abortionist. Go to those who have tried every avenue open to science in order to become parents, and find they cannot have children.) The other precept follows it, "A little child shall lead them. . . ." Of course there are wider meanings than the specific directive for which I am using these precepts. Proofs for them cannot be found in any divorce court or action; rather, the proof lies in quiet, undramatic lives to which we give too little heed.

To stay married because of a firm belief in such principles takes the burden away from the children! The stress that leads to thoughts of escape or divorce may not be easily or quickly resolved, and children of preschool age are nonetheless sensitive to variations of mood, affection and temper, whether repressed or expressed; yet built into such couples' stick-to-it-iveness, there is a standard of behavior which the children understand, even wordlessly, and will one day imitate. The fact that no words indicate perception or understanding does not negate the fact that such children learn that adult behavior does not arise from variations of mood or circumstance, but from principles which do not fluctuate. Thus stress with its natural fluctuations is not the threat that it is to those who see in their moods a "cause" for change of life-direction. Steadiness and endurance are taught by the most powerful of teaching methods to such children, that is, by example. Above all, such children know themselves to be valued, not for appearances, or talent, or obedience, but for a transcendence which links them to a divinity they may not comprehend, but which becomes a generational gift passed on from parent to child.

To stay married "for the sake of the children" is a burden only when the child is invested with emotions which should be directed toward the mate. However, since this is not a would/should relationship, couples considering divorce and yet remaining married must take careful note of these tendencies within themselves. Even in a home where romantic love has ceased to exist, substitution and sublimation can be practiced. But such lives can only succeed if parents are motivated by the recognition of a love that is greater than a love for self. It is by no means the accepted Hollywood criteria for love, nor is it psychologically masochistic. Both of these popular concepts must be resisted. Love greater than self is a stern dictum, and few care to embark upon it. At first glance it may seem to be "a need to suffer." In fact, it is in the spirit of Christ's definition, "Greater love hath no man than this, that a man lay down his life for his friends" (John 15:3). It is redeemed from all taints of masochism, regardless of psychological interpretations because it is a *willed renunciation* based on a principle that in no way places a burden on the children involved.

Parents tempted to divorce are passing through what we may term the *adolescence* of marriage. It is a deteriorating relationship of lost excitement. Time is its author and finisher, and lost excitement is a difficult thing to give up. Some people never will give it up, and delude themselves with each successive mate by descriptions that invariably claim, "But this one is not like any of the others!" And by virtue of *difference* an identical set of expectations is set in motion, until time tests the mettle of it. That which was once satisfied *by* the mate or *through* the mate has reached a plateau of dailiness, of sameness. For some, *change* is found threatening. Unfortunately, the simple fact is given other labels than change. Disappointment can find any number of specific flaws to summon as rationales for a yet larger change, namely, divorce.

We believe, and rightly so, that we were created for variety. Does not the infinite variety of the universe itself imply our need? Certainly it does. But this is not true where parenthood is concerned. As surely as we are of this earth, equally changeless and immutable is the bond between parent and child, and it allows for no variation or change. True, the externals of parenthood may change. When a parent dies, there are surrogate parents who may be finer in all respects than the actual blood-parent, yet the blood-relationship is never changed. A child can accept what is inevitable in death, but a subtle difference exists where one parent arbitrarily bestows on a child another father or mother through the channels of divorce. An innate sense of the "rightness" of things is shattered in the child. Any child heard saying, "But he's not my *real* father" is paying tribute to the immutability of the blood-bond.

Yet there is something egotistical and repugnant about anyone who is heard saying, "I lay down my life for these children." Therefore, it should not, indeed, cannot, be spoken without losing its efficacy. The laid-down life can only be lived. It cannot look for praise or reward during its term of tenure. Moreover, the laid-down life of a parent finds its truest and best description when it is viewed by a child who has lived its benefits, a child who has reached adulthood and can view it without mawkish sentiment. Such a one has internalized the stern lesson of parental sacrifice and experienced its beauties and rewards.

To lay down one's life in a changing marriage from which the first benefits, and perhaps even the first joys, have flown, involves a redirection of attention, an emphasis deflected from personal happiness, in complete assurance that a new happiness will be found. How? In giving first priority to the well-being of another, specifically, our children. This sets in motion a self-forgetfulness which carries as a by-product a paradoxical happiness. The course of "greater love" has rewards as well as the support of other truths.

The path *is* Christ-like and psychologically healthy. It is emotionally healthy in that it reinforces the mature skill of delayed gratification which raises humans above the status of animals. This is most distasteful to the modern mind, programed as we are to a huge array of "instant" gratifications. Substitution and sublimation become a continual form of self-discipline which teaches the children of such a relationship the meaning of endurance, and passes on a high frustration tolerance through which a higher kind of happiness is attained.

It may well be asked, "Are children a sufficient dynamic for the laying down of personal aims?" By no means. Again, it *is* a burden no child should be called upon to bear. The dynamic which makes the laid-down life palatable and workable is that it has the support of time-tested proofs. The promise: "He that loveth his life will lose it" (John 12:25), ". . . whosoever will lose his life for my sake, the same shall save it" (Luke 9:24).

Such a dynamic takes the basis for the action away from the children's needs. A belief in, and an obedience to, a principle that one's life is never lost in voluntarily sacrificing it becomes, therefore, a dynamic of faith. Out of such "loss" we find our real selfhood.

Although little research and little communication exists in the outworking of this principle in marriage, persons in the united home are no less subject to fluctuating circumstances, moods, and the perennial need for escape that afflicts divorcing couples. The difference lies in the rewards and supports built into the sacrificed self.

Long-term marriages in which every material advantage is granted are seen to be breaking up. This fact should tell us how tormenting and how long-lasting can be the desire for escape. It has been stated for us in a poem by King David: "Oh that I had wings like a dove! for then would I fly away, and be at rest" (Ps. 55:6). In the context of marriage in a modern age, none of us can live without the contagion and contamination of such wishes. The truthful will freely admit they are not superior for remaining married. They simply accept a restraint imposed by truths they humbly accept.

A woman once divorced married a second mate and found herself once again with a lifetime desire for separation from her second husband. Each time she came to a decision for divorce, she remembered her Teacher's words, ". . . whoever causes one of these little ones to . . . sin[stumble], it would be better for him to have a great millstone fastened round his neck and to be drowned in the depth of the sea" (Matt. 18:6). Would her escape create a "door" for other divorces? Would her escape put a stumbling block in the way of "little ones" she loved? She accepted the fact that divorce begets divorce and decided, "This cycle has to end with me." What happened? Presently, at age eighty-five, she has found a sustaining factor. The promise which upheld her Teacher has upheld her. With wrinkled hands on her Bible, she smiles at the certain truth of the words: ". . . who for the joy that was set before him endured the cross . . ." (Heb. 12:2). Is she waiting for some mystical pie-in-the-sky satisfaction? No, hers is an old age not very different from that of the old patriarchs. Hers is a strength that can say with Caleb who said in his eightieth year, "Give me this mountain," secure in the fact that the Master he served *had* sustained and *would* sustain (Josh. 14:12).

Were this mother's talents wasted? Were energies that could have been directed toward other goals uselessly sacrificed? No, she was given the gift of a long and fruitfully fulfilled life. Her example of voluntary self-sacrifice saved countless other marriages from divorce. In the midst of a crooked and perverse generation, she preserved the sanctity of the home. She learned to be long-suffering *with joyfulness!*

Nothing was wasted. Every talent was put to account in a way that could not have proved true had she placed personal development first.

What begins as a resolve to sacrifice the life becomes a transcending act that by-passes the circumstances of human marital differences and even the needs of children, until endurance is attributed to a daily acceptance of the principle: "God first."

And from a daily dependence on God, there comes a

re-direction of energies *to* God for the sake of others, which transforms any marriage. It should be asked, "In what specific way does this transform any marriage?" By making even one member of a marriage an instrument of peace. But in *all* cases, one cannot make such a sacrifice without the dynamic of God's enabling. Nor is it necessary for both parties in a marriage to be of like persuasion. Ideally, it should be so, but rarely is it the case. One believing half of the two who are married brings God's presence into that relationship and sanctifies both mate and children. St. Paul puts it even more strongly; it sanctifies the *unbelieving* mate (1 Cor. 7:14)!

Where there is hatred there will be a love totally unlike the love we read in novels, or which appears in Hollywood movies. It will be a love which covers faults. Where faults cannot be taken away, the function of love is to hide them; to cover the blemish; to excuse; to pardon the failing. Once? No, until seventy times seven. That member will become an instrument of daily pardon, knowing his own daily pardon is conditioned by his pardon of his own family. Where there is doubt, there will be the rewards of faith. Where there is despair, there will always be hope. Where there is darkness, light will be given. Where there is sadness, joy will come.

Contrary to logic? No, St. Paul was the most logical of men, trained under that master logician, Gamaliel. He tells us, ". . . present your *bodies*, a living sacrifice, . . . that ye may prove what is that good, and acceptable, and perfect, will of God." How? "And . . . be ye transformed by the renewing of your mind" (Romans 12:1-2).

The answer is simple, but it is an exercise in severe self-discipline which involves a life of daily *mental renewal.*

17

Mother-In-Law or Mother-In-Love?

The cure for all the ills and wrongs,
the cares, the sorrows, and the crimes
of humanity, all lie in that one word
"love." It is the divine vitality that
everywhere produces and restores life.
To each and every one of us, it gives the
power of working miracles if we will. (Mrs. L.M. Child)

Would there be so many jokes about the mother-in-law if there were no truth in them? Why do they persist? With the breakdown of the family, there is also an increased emphasis on the repressed hostilities beneath the laughing witticism of such jokes. Obviously, we can ignore the jokes and cartoons, but we should examine the underlying causes.

Meanwhile, we have built more enduring monuments than the passing mother-in-law joke. Our dislike for our parents, mothers, and mothers-in-law are architecturally made permanent. Of course, we never see these buildings as "monuments." They are instead euphemistically referred to as Old Ladies' *Homes*, Nursing *Homes*, Dun Roving, Valhalla, Pine Haven, Lakeside Hall, Loch Lomond Manor, and a host of verbal sugar coating. Superlatives are added. We promise the ultimate in "personalized, warm care." In fine print, we place the prison terms, "custodial," "rehabilitation" and "therapy." Then we bring in the government with the assurance of "registered nurses" and "medicare benefits." We are urged to consider that "a visit justifies a decision." Yet there is nothing to conceal the fact that we look upon aging as a process which must be segregated from the mainstream of life.

But aging is not the focus of this exploration. We become mothers-in-law so gradually that we see no change in ourselves, or in our status in a changing society. Moreover, it so natural we sense no visible transition except in the marriage ceremony of our son or our daughter. Perhaps, as is common in today's world, the physical move from home to his or her own apartment signals the change of status if son or daughter chooses to live in the "one-flesh" relationship without the ritual or formality of marriage. Regardless of its social form, you as a parent must face the dictum laid down by the ancients: "For this cause shall a man [person] leave his father and mother, and shall cleave to his wife [her mate] and they twain shall be one flesh" (Matt. 19:5).

In any case, they are no longer under your control or direction, be that gentle-handed, generous-handed, or overbearing. Perhaps you had no recognition of your own powers until they were tested by adolescent rebellion and its gradual emergence into adult independence? After the adolescent testing of powers, their trial "run" at independence of parents, it is often a distinct pleasure when the parent senses the inner independence that is taking form. It is well to call to mind one's own "declarations of freedom" from parental rule. Often it may be college or job opportunities which precipitate a personal independence; other times it may be marriage.

When your daughter brings "him" home, it is usually the father whose every instinct is alert to the most subtle nuances in the young man's personality and character. If the father was a philanderer in his youth, he will be suspicious of almost any young man his daughter dates. He will objectify his own "wild oats," or project his own fantasies on to his daughter's intended. In parallel fashion, a mother whose own marriage has been unhappy will attach fear for her daughter's happiness to her reception of the young couple. The wonder is not that there are so many divorces; the miracle continues to lie in the marriages that endure. Burdened with their parents' projections, the sheer optimism of the young is clear evidence of human transcendence of their parents' dire predictions.

The mother of the daughter often errs in wanting for her daughter all that she did not have. Whatever the older woman's disappointments may be, she will, directly or indirectly, pass them on to her daughter. Did she marry a poor man? She will tell her daughter that it as easy to love a rich man as a poor man. Has she had a lifetime of "giving-in"? She will plant the seeds of, "Don't let him talk you into" or "Nip it in the bud the first weeks of your marriage." On the other hand, if, at the outset of the romance, the mother states unequivocably, "He's no good!" and the marriage takes place, the ordinary adjustments of married life will be magnified by that nagging suggestion. Maybe mom was right? Maybe he is no good? Maybe love *is* blind? Meanwhile, the husband senses the calculations, the "on-trial" atmosphere of his wife's parents. It requires no great insight to understand that a young husband being so criticized, so scrutinized, so evaluated will make the very errors of which he is suspected. The "climate" of psychological expectation with which he is surrounded, in the people who are intensely important to his wife, will wreak its inevitable havoc in the young married couple.

Small wonder that we have comic strips, cartoons, movies and television jokes about the stereotyped mother-in-law. Nonetheless, truths which keep them alive and perpetuate them should be examined. They *can* be exposed and exorcised by parental education as well as by marital counseling.

What about the husband's mother? Is it perhaps a more intense parallel than that which exists between father and daughter? When Moses at God's direction wrote of women, he said, "Your desire shall be to your husband" (Gen. 3:16), the implication extends to the deep maternal tenderness a woman feels toward her baby son. Such feelings cannot be directed to her husband; husband and wife are, ideally, too equal. She meets his passion with her own desires; his energies are met with a feminine complementary strength; his mind evokes sparks from her own. But here, in the person of her baby son, is a *helpless* male who draws from her a well of tenderness and a range of complicated feelings that the full grown male neither needs nor evokes. In return, the little boy finds in his mother what he will later seek in a wife. All his latent maleness is contained in his three-year-old, "Oh, mommy, I wuv you!" This may give way to, "When I get big, can I marry you?" Later, the affectionate boy may hear, "Mama's boy! Mama's boy!" and immediately all demonstrative gestures of affection towards his mother are in danger. If he is unsure of his masculinity, he may never resume the greeting's kiss. If his masculinity is a thing in which he is assured, he will return the affectionate hug for mom, secure in his recognition that his sexually-oriented demonstrativeness toward his wife is distinct from a son's maternal bonds.

It is the mother who has the greatest potential for transgression here. When she held her term of cradle-rule, the day for the severing of apron strings seemed far removed. She may find herself unprepared for that total transfer of affections from herself to another woman. Again, this is more intense if she, herself, has transferred her marital discontents to an emotional dependence on her son.

It is not the place or calling of the young wife to have the emotional insights that a longer life should grant. It should be the older woman, in all cases, who makes the efforts to accept and understand and to love. In that order, a mother of a son or daughter must learn to accept "as is" whomever her adult children choose to love. The older woman begins with total acceptance. A mere act of will, a tacit respect for the *feelings* of her own offspring is what this amounts to. After acceptance comes understanding, and with understanding comes genuine love. Not love as it is cinematically portrayed, but love that wants only the well-being of its object. Nor can she "want" this well-being in any directive manner. It must be a "hands-off" love.

Can one love someone for whom there may not be any natural affinity? Can one love where love is not wanted, where the young person (man or woman) visibly resents the older person? Yes, it is possible to love one who positively rejects your love, if we understand that dislike and rejection are actually a sign of fear and self-hate. When this is understood, it is possible to have compassion for the sense of unworthiness from which such people must suffer; a disinterested love follows. This is a love which strives to understand that each one of us shares similar joys, sufferings, ideas, needs. It is the task of the older woman to remember her own sense of inadequacy in the early stages of the love relationship, to remember that the love we share is by its very nature also a vehicle for pain at the characters, judgments, faculties and ideals that are so often different in spite of the love that unites us.

However, it is easy to deceive ourselves that we love in a sweeping assumption that we hate no one. This is self-complacency. When we speak of loving the unlovely, or those who actively dislike us, we must step beyond humanistic love. In order to do this, we must accept the fact that we are loved by God "even when we were His enemies," loved to the uttermost degradation, regardless of whether we were worthy or unworthy. When we have internalized this, the commandment to love becomes easy, and it becomes a fact that, "We know that we have passed from death unto life, because we love [one another]" (1 John 3:14). We need not respond to rejection in kind; we can identify with the love that chose us before we could respond, and take the initiative in loving. To be mothers-in-love is as great a miracle as the miracle of actual mothers-by-birth.

18

The Alcoholic Spouse or Family Member

It is easy, terribly easy,
to shake a man's faith in himself.
To take advantage of that
to break a man's spirit
is devil's work.
(Candide: George Bernard Shaw)

The nondrinker in the family situation is in almost as much "danger" as the alcoholic. That danger is ignorance. Plato's claim that "it is better to be unborn than to be untaught" is perhaps nowhere more applicable than in the area of problem drinking, for the nondrinker does not begin to comprehend the compulsion which lies at the roots of alcoholism.

Since there is hardly a family anywhere in the world which is not intimately or distantly "touched" by alcoholism, removing the secrecy with which nondrinkers surround it should be our first step in examining the problem.

But the secrecy has its roots in a sense of shame. And where does the shame in a nondrinker originate? If such a one does not drink, why is he ashamed? Obviously, there could be no shame if there were no guilt, and the guilt arises from the ramifications and ambiguities of the love-hate feelings aroused in almost anyone who does *not* drink. I refer to those who see only the indignity, the brutality, the horror that often accompanies the alcoholic problem.

One example may serve to amplify the presence of guilt in the nondrinking family member. Upon returning to her home one night, a wife found her husband drunk and asleep on a bed which had been set afire by a lighted cigarette. Without apparent thought, she speedily extinguished the fire and saved both her husband and her home. However, she confesses the temptation which was hers in the very act of saving her husband. The ugly hope that he would be dead was in her heart as she beat out the flames. Such accounts have as many variations as there are varieties of human experience. Deeds too terrible to tell have been done under the influence of drunkenness; fear, anger, bitterness, resentment, self-pity and hate are aroused in the sober family members.

Ignorance in the nondrinking observer gives way to disgust, and angry accusation, hot-tempered responses, reproaches and even physical abuse are frequently aroused in the sober partner. It is a well-guarded secret that it is the tiny, ninety pound, nondrinking wife who breaks a chair over her stumbling drunken husband's head. Of course, the alcoholic may have gone to far greater lengths in physical violence, but if truth is to exercise its liberating function, it must also expose the violence aroused in sober family members. At this stage the blame-game reaches its zenith. Frequently the only "out" for the nondrinker is to cite the laws of cause and effect, namely, that for every action there is a reaction equal in intensity. The sober member cites the fact that in the face of atrocious behavior, anger is inevitable. On the other hand, if the alcoholic has a foggy recollection, his heavy hangover now has a target in a person, rather than in his last drink. This is the moral level of mutual guilt on which both nondrinker and alcoholic meet on equal footing, though neither will acknowledge the fact.

A nondrinker's explosion may give temporary relief, and he excuses his violence on such grounds as defense or provocation. If such people are religiously inclined, they will summon Christ's cleansing of the temple as their rationale and self-righteously repress all guilt at their own loss of self-control. Clearly, the guilt continues to operate, and the family "climate" of the continuing blame-game is self-perpetuated.

Insidiously, the nondrinker finds a source of strength in indignation. A "catalog of grievances" nourishes the bruised ego, and perspective is lost. A "holier-than-thou" atmosphere causes all family members to live with distorted self-images, because the "reality" of the situation is faced by neither the alcoholic nor the "sober" members. However, retaliation on the part of the nondrinker should give him a glimpse of the depths of irrationality within the human heart. His own response of burning hate should lead him to say with St. Paul, "*I* am the chief of sinners" (1 Tim. 1:15). If this could be said after long years of serving his Lord, it must be on this starkly realistic base that a genuine self-image rests. Moreover, the nondrinker must acknowledge that the evil in his own heart and impulses are there without the compulsion to drink. Not until each one of us can look at any human derelict and say without parroting or mouthing, "There, but for the grace of God go I," are we prepared to take the first step toward what is a family problem: alcoholism.

First, what is the nature of alcohol? It is a chemical and, like medically administered chemicals given by doctors in the nature of sedation (such as valium or librium), human behavior changes *are due to the nature of the substance.* Alcohol never changes its properties. It acts as an anesthetic. (It once was medically used as such.) The nervous system is turned off in anyone who drinks! It is also true that alcohol is not digested, but is directly absorbed through the stomach lining into the bloodstream where it spreads through the system in twenty-two seconds by way of the circulatory process. The degree to which one is affected depends on such additives as food and one's physical condition.

Acting as a depressant, alcohol affects the brain's discretionary centers first. The drinker says, "How a drink relaxes me!" This is not psychological; it is due to the anesthetic properties of ethyl alcohol. Thus the withdrawn person may become the life of the party, or the outgoing gregarious person may retreat into "unnatural" silence. What was once controlled by the judgment, i.e., the discretionary part of the brain, is turned off by alcohol. The "high risk" group, among social drinkers, are those who do not feel anything after many drinks. Why are such people more susceptible? Because alcohol is a toxic substance and the body's detoxification organ is the liver, and the body develops a tolerance. Since the liver can only process one ounce or less of alcohol per hour, the so-called "good" drinker is in the most dangerous position. Obviously, the ability to take many drinks without apparent effect indicates a body which does not reject the toxic substance, though it is well known that drinking while eating retards the body's absorption process to such an extent that one may not *feel* the effects.

Again, the person under the influence of alcohol does not understand that he is drunk any more than the person under anesthesia comprehends his own reactions. Quite naturally the drinker thinks his family is "against him."

Since discretionary centers of the brain are "hit," the drinker passes through the stages of loss of inhibitions, tone-of-voice changes, belligerence, in which the decision to "get their goat" is made. Finally, the depressant reaches the center of motor control and the drinker staggers and accidents occur. At times, this saturation point can be a form of protection in which the involuntary motor system is affected and the drinker "passes out." But this does not stop the absorption process; alcohol in the body continues to be absorbed. It must also be remembered that alcohol is an anti-food which contains 150 calories per ounce, yet it has no nutritional value. Therefore, the drinker's calories stifle the hunger drive and he eats less. At the same time, the body's nutritional needs remain unmet. Gastritis and pancreaitis are among the effects. A solvent, alcohol can eat a hole in the finish of a table, and does the same thing to the lining of the stomach until the stage is reached where nothing is more repulsive than eating.

Like diabetes, alcoholism is a *chronic* disease. It is chronic in that it will never go away—ever! The diabetic will never be able to say, "I *had* diabetes." They recognize that they can *never* tolerate wrong substances. Similarly, the alcoholic cannot tolerate mind-changing medicines. Alcoholics are, in fact, seditavists and are thus allergic to all nervous system medication. Their only "cure" lies in total abstinence.

Tragically, alcohol-related deaths are often listed as cirrhosis of the liver and heart failure. Among the ten million alcholics in the United States, fewer than 10 percent recover; the remaining 90 percent die or are put away.*

---

* Based on notes from: Alina Lodge Alcoholic Rehabilitation Center, Blairstown, New Jersey (Highest "recovery" rate in U.S.)

19

The Nondrinker's "Danger"

*Judge not, lest you be judged;
for with what measure you mete
it shall be measured unto you again.
(Matt. 7:1)*

*God help me to accept my powerlessness
over alcohol and its effects. I will direct
my efforts to improving the one life
over which I do have power, my own.
(Alcoholics Anonymous)*

Cynically, the "sober" spouse protests, "Don't dignify drunkenness by calling it a disease!" To answer the protest, what are the criteria by which human aberrations may be labeled diseases? Easily recognized are diseases of the anatomy such as fractures, lacerations and the like. Organic malfunction such as cancer and diabetes are also accepted as diseases. Since alcohol resembles diabetes, research is being conducted to ascertain whether there is a predisposition to alcohol. Is it hereditary?

A third criterion for disease is emotional or psychological imbalance, which may be chemically induced. But we tend to see alcoholism as a result, not as a cause. We look for personality disorders and see drinking as a symptom. Hence, a serious misdiagnosis could well be what we call schizophrenia, which may be due to alcohol. A chemically induced imbalance, alcohol destroys the will power until the compulsion to drink demands that a person do what he does not want to do. Alcohol is in control, not the will; the controlling mechanism is lost, yet total abstinence is not the sole answer. There must be a *change in all areas*, and *abstinence is the prerequisite* for those changes. It follows that the first step for drinker and nondrinker in the family situation must be the total admission of helplessness in the face of what is, in fact, a disease. Unfortunately, too many of us accept the cliche, "God helps those who help themselves." This is a false platitude. St. Paul, St. Augustine and every member of Alcoholics Anonymous and its related organizations for families of alcoholics (Al-Anon, Al-A-Teen), know that God does *not* help those who help themselves in the area of drinking. How do these hosts of people know this? They have tried it. But St. Paul said it for all of us. "[The] will is present with me; but how to perform that which is good I find not. For the good that I would I do not: but the evil which I would not, that I do" (Rom. 7:18-19). Even more than the alcoholic, all so-called "good" people should recollect the countless times they have set their wills and failed to follow through. We must all admit with St. Augustine that there are areas in the human psyche in which, "The mind will not obey the mind."

But the concept of self-sufficiency is the last belief we adults will reject. We cite our autonomy, our inner-directedness, our ability to adapt, our ability to hold responsible positions, all of which are a far cry from powerlessness and helplessness. Wise as we may claim to be, we must admit our complete helplessness against alcoholism.

If, as A.A. states, the alcoholic must "hit bottom" before helplessness will be admitted, it is even more difficult for the clear-headed, logical, efficient nondrinker to admit to the same helplessness. Again, it is precisely with this admission that our hopes for the family survival must meet and unite. This admission is, as A.A. states it, the *first* step. Step two follows it. We come to believe that God is the answer to our helplessness, and in humility, whose earmarks are a childlike dependency, we learn to turn our powerlessness over to Him. But never think that this is easy. Self-sufficiency in the nondrinker is nearly as strong a deterrent as alcohol is to the alcoholic. To affirm our faith in God through acknowledged helplessness is merely a prelude to another stage; a point at which we lay aside all right to a personal independence, and say with our lips, while we act out in actual life, "Thy will, not mine, be done."

Nonetheless, in a very brief time, we learn that our mental and emotional independence asserts itself. The old egotism takes over and we make our former personally determined decisions. To get out from under the tyranny of self and/or alcohol, we add a fourth step, that of continuous self-examination. Or, as A.A. puts it, "a searching and fearless moral inventory."

Business concerns recognize the need for regular inventory; they know it must be a continuous process for as long as a firm is in business. How much more necessary it is to take stock of the shelves and closets of human character. We begin with those humanly shared seven: pride, greed, lust, anger, gluttony, envy, sloth. How fitting that pride heads the list, for pride wears the disguise of self-respect and self-righteousness, and it always comes in the guise of something good. Little wonder it has been called the "queen of sins."

In the context of marriage, pride is adept at saying as Adam said, "The woman *you* gave is at fault. I did not eat that apple because of any wrong in me!" Blame is pride's first weapon. In the area of personal inventory, pride will block the way to self-examination with a long list of self-justifying excuses. Adam's excuse is shared by women as well as men. "Because of my mate, I must do thus and so." Pride is the master of the alibi. Why? Because, if we drop the word "blame," our fear of losing that comfortable security of a target other than self would leave us face to face with failings we habitually place on "others."

How then do we proceed? Because the outward life of the nondrinker may reveal no serious defects, such a one is more reluctant than the alcoholic to dig under a lifetime's layers of self-righteousness. Unlike the alcoholic who has alienated family and friends with his drinking, who may even have lost his job security, the nondrinker sees himself in a dangerously favorable light. Let us take it out of the context of alcoholism and remember that great teacher, Socrates, who said, "The unexamined life is not worth living." From this vantage point, we know that a liberal education is one of the finest ways in which to pursue "the examined life." Through the study of literature or philosophy, we are enabled to examine a thousand lives and draw inferences and parallels relevant to our own lives.

Another way in which to examine one's life is to write out questions and answers. If one has been self-deceptive and less than honest, a rereading after a passage of time will reveal it to us. But the mere fact of writing will assist in clarifying our thinking and give evidence of our willingness to *try* the moral inventory.

The most thorough path to self-examination is laid down by the injunction, "Confess your faults one to another . . . that ye may be healed" (James 5:16). This places the verbalizing of our own faults on a high level. Indeed, this shows that the emphasis is not on the confessor, but on the *act* of confession. This is also the function of psychoanalysis. Too many people attribute a mystique of omnipotence to the analyst, whereas in essence, successful analysis helps us to help ourselves. The analyst does not solve the problems brought to him. It is in the very act of verbalizing a problem that the patient solves his own problem. Some of the repugnancy expressed by visitors to A.A. or Al-Anon concerns this free, and apparently easy, public talk about personal defects. "I can't stand all of the rehashing of personal liabilities, especially such private affairs!" says one. But this display of psychic nudity is for the purpose of clearing away fear of self-examination in the newcomer. Persons eager to be helped are reassured that they, too, can look at their own defects without fear. Thus, listening to painful and humiliatingly frank disclosures on the part of others grants a perspective on our own defects.

"Why can't I confess my wrongs to God alone? Doesn't the Bible say we have an Advocate with God in Christ? Doesn't it also say the Spirit itself makes intercession for us with groanings which cannot be uttered? Surely that is enough?"

No, it is too easy for us to delude ourselves when we are alone with God. We have ample witnesses to the fact that people with the best of intentions have been mistaken in what they claim God has told them. The saints themselves have left us records concerning the need for spiritual superiors in the areas of healing and guidance.

Above all, a personal inventory acts as an emotional catharsis. If our daily intake of food demands the regular evacuation of bowels, how much more regular should be the evacuation of cumulative negative emotions! Every day our lives interact with other human beings; conditions over which we have no control require endless adaptation. Therefore, any symptoms of worry, anger, self-pity and depression should be "ventilated" in order that they may be dissipated. It is good to begin this process by asking where we ourselves have been at fault, and why, because this directs our thinking away from "blame" and the easy pitfalls of projection.

More than anything else, a lifetime's practice in self-inventory results in daily renewal of spiritual, mental, and physical energies. Above all, it fulfills the command, "Be transformed by the renewing of your mind."

20

Grandparents on the Sidelines of Divorce

Because of one small head
of golden hair,
All little heads forevermore
a halo wear. (Anon.)

"Of course we never see our grandchildren," she said matter-of-factly. I nodded as if I understood perfectly. But who except those who are denied such joys can really understand? Through our children we find the feeling that we are part of the work of creation, but in our children's children there is no danger of turning that love into dependence. Instead, grandparents represent stability and continuity, and ideally, they should pass on a residue of peace and enthusiasm after the conflicts of a longer life. There should be generational gifts that reflect another era passed on from grandma and grandpa to the little ones. Different interests and different needs can be explored without either group being threatened. A climate of give and take in the accepting tolerance of old age will give children a greater feeling of family solidarity than where no grandparents exist. Above all, grandparents have the *time*, or should have, to draw out potentials in their grandchildren that busy, preoccupied parents have not the leisure to grant.

But I am speaking of a till-death-do-us-part generation, and the fact that my friend was describing the details of her son's divorce was something of a breakdown of reserve.

While we might mention divorce as one speaks of the weather, details are more often omitted. But when divorce becomes the dilemma of our own children, the attitude of grandparents will be largely determined by their own frame of reference, their cultural heritage, and personal "hang-ups."

As older people, grandparents should be experienced enough in living to know the power of strong feelings. Child rearing should have taught them not to take sides. Their own marriages should show them that in the breakdown of any marriage, there are faults on *both* sides, their own included.

Can grandparents be detached without being indifferent? Very often all one's parent-feelings will come to the fore, and one will begin to enumerate in thought all the faults of the marital partner who is not your son or your daughter. A long marriage, if it is an honest one, will show that there is always failure on both sides.

Grandparents must resist all inclinations to enter the arena of the blame-game. This must begin with an open admission of how vengeful their own hearts can be where flesh and blood are threatened. Once the battle with self is examined and not disowned, one is freed from the spirit of blame. We are able to affirm that in *every* human relationship, we must accept the other "as is." The least vestige of nonacceptance will be sensed by the "other," to the detriment of all. Just as the doctor and lawyer disqualify themselves where their own families are involved, in like fashion grandparents should recognize that they can be neither matter-of-fact nor resigned. The ache to see those fleeting expressions that childhood's growing can never duplicate will awake a fierce longing. Those stages in the lives of little children are able to turn back the clock of time in such a way that all our first-time parental tenderness makes a mawkish poem reveal a dimension of truth that is wholly surprising. "Backward, turn backward, O Time, in your flight." Uncomprehendingly, our grandchildren pass before us in exact duplication of some grown-up who was once little for such a little while!

But when our own were, in fact, babies, there were nights of little or no sleep—nights when you kept the croup kettle's moisture going all night (and the kettles were not automatic as they are today). Nights when your nerves were finely strung to hear the slightest murmur of change in a tiny chest that your hand could span. You could clearly hear the wetness in those tiny lungs. You could hear the waving of miniscule fingers against miniature sheets. At such times you might think, or even say, "I'll be glad when he's big enough to walk, then I'll know he's strong."

When the first baby word is spoken you discover that "da-da" is easier than "ma-ma" for those baby lips to frame. I liked the idea of the seed-bearer getting first honors. It took nothing away from my sense of equality. In the equation of creation, I have no quarrel with feminine passivity. No fanfare or parade of intellect will change the fact that *I am the receiver* of that seed. As such, a complementary hierarchy is implied, and not even cloning will change for me.

To the two parents, first baby words are magic. And the magic remains for any baby. The wonder of attaching meaning to sound will always remain a miracle. An added revelation is the fact that there is as much magic in the words of the last child as there is in the first.

When I had my first baby I thought that surprising rush of tenderness could never be repeated, but it returns with all its first-time yearning. The circumstances of economics in the first year of marriage did not favor pregnancy, but I believed with all my heart that "Children *are* an inheritance from God." The first sight of my little one was a rapture all gentled by the fragility of what it looked upon! It came as a surprise. One tried for planned parenthood in those days, but often pregnancy was shadowed by melancholy parents who saw life in terms of some terrible burden. A mother's sorrowful remark about her son as a young father was, "Poor man, now he will have both feet in this world." It was evident in her mind that the advent of a child marked the beginning of some burdensome future. Other parents, speaking out of grinding poverty will say, "You're not going to have any more children, I hope?" It was impossible for such attitudes not to have an effect on a young pregnant mother experiencing her unwieldy body for the first time. It followed that at birth, I was totally unprepared for that surge of most tender love, as I timidly drew a finger over the tea-cup sized face so newly released from my own body. What had ever felt so vulnerably soft? I was suddenly all protective joy, and life was all renewal.

When I tried to put these feelings into words, an older woman said harshly, "It will pass!" And, of course, it passed into memory, which is not to say it disappeared. At eleven, my sons could be arrogantly protective of me, and I delighted as much in their precocious manliness and gallantry as I had delighted in their infancy. Their sturdy reassurances, "Don't worry, mom!" in a storm when our little rowboat was in danger of capsizing, gave me no wish to return them to their babyhood. Rather, I was proud of their independence. The superiority they evidenced in wanting to protect me was a sweet token of their sense of strength in meeting other storms, and of my own femininity in their eyes. A strong woman is not immune to out-dated courtliness; it should be brought back!

When he became a father, one of my sons made certain that I saw his new son at the same time as he himself saw him. Not a word was spoken between us. The nurse said for us, "He is the image of his daddy!" At once there was a new comprehension in the eyes of my son. Was it an "intimation of immortality"? Though it was another woman's child, the little one seemed mine twice-given! I thought of the word *grand*, and paused to take it in. My twice-given ones are more than any synonym for "grand." True, they cannot be called magnificent, august, noble, illustrious or stately except in the sense that every child exceeds the magnificence of royalty itself. In my mother tongue the word is not "grand," it is "child's child," and grandmother is called, "father's mother" or "mother's mother" or the "best-mother." But in our first look, that secret surge of tenderness was there again with all its ache of love.

The day came when there were eight twice-given children's children. In the holiday pandemonium, little ones made themselves felt. Busy adult members of the family began to say we were too many to come together all at the same time, but I loved it.

My profession demanded that preparations for family holidays be made far in advance, but this merely added to my efficiency. To have the Christmas shopping done by July for a family of eighteen was no super-task; it granted time for moments of stillness at a season too often flawed by hurry and impatience. The noise and confusion were vitality and laughter when they were juxtaposed with the gift of unhurry which I had given myself in shopping ahead. When other grandparents said, "I'm glad to see them come, but I'm also glad to see them go," we agreed that babies were for youthful parents. The heart's home longs to keep them, while aging bodies and nerves cannot keep up with the affection's inclinations.

Nonetheless, there is a transfer of energy that overflows from youth to age, just as there should be total acceptance, calmness and patience for age to transmit to youth. These are not qualities which must be passed on verbally, but are best exchanged by osmosis, and the mere fact of being in each other's presence.

A wealth of multiplied experiences are shared by children who have loving grandparents. Like anticipated holidays, grandparents should be sprinkled lightly over the life of our children's children. There should be simple, but enduring memories of "special holidays." These need not be an unvarying diet of happy holidays; family sharing should include the human spectrum of sadness, anger, fear, illness, tenderness, and joy. Shared experiences grant an enlarged heart that will later open to a wide variety of responses. The intimacy of shared family gatherings becomes an important bulwark against a future separation. Such children may grow to an adulthood in which they are parted from their families by continents, yet wherever such a one goes he will never be really alone. He is and remains a part of a *family*.

Specifically, how should grandparents on the sidelines of divorce conduct themselves? First, resist the impulse to assign "blame." If your daughter's husband leaves her for another woman, or beats her, or deserts her, how can that be met without blame? Yet no one is helped if we *add* to their sense of injury. Instead, every effort should be made to strengthen her for independence; sympathy will serve sadly to augment her self-pity. Listening without comment will enable her to sort out the erupting volcano of her own feelings. Above all, the terrible treachery and deceitfulness of the heart's inclinations should never be forgotten. For example, husband A went "off with another woman," leaving four very young children behind. Both the husband and the wife were supported by parents who vociferously added their own indignation to the problems of the battling pair. The daughter's father became so embroiled, he had a cerebral hemorrhage and died. Four years later the couple remarried.

Is this an account which concerns ignorant or uneducated people? No, all parties, parents as well as the divorcing pair, were college graduates. Who can know the deeply private and personal ramifications of such tangles? Indeed, it is not necessary that such privacies be exhumed. To all observers, the healed marriage is now of ten years duration, but the "root of bitterness" which the older generation of grandparents nourished and kept alive has caused a deeper rift in family unity than the legal divorce which was undone by the renewed commitment of remarriage. Anger need leave no bitter roots if it is neutralized by pardon.

Again, grandparent's attitudes will be determined by their frame of reference. A member of that generation now in her eighties spent twenty-five years of her divorced life "giving the old man a hard time." Meanwhile, to comfort her in her bitterness, a favorite granddaughter spent long and frequent visits with her. No one now questions the parallel which has taken place. Oddly, that same young girl has grown up to perpetuate, for more than a decade, the same behavior toward her own husband that her grandmother practiced toward her grandfather. Clearly, we pass on to others much more than we recognize. This is especially true of bitterness and anger. Younger people who follow will imitate on the subconscious assumption that grandma, with so many years behind her, *must* be right.

Yet this is not to say that grandparents should retreat from all involvement. They should take the initiative in loving, even when loving is difficult and painful. We cannot expect to be automatically loved because we are parents and grandparents, as if we should have all the rewards without giving anything of ourselves to the relationship. Above all, out of a longer life, grandparents should give a love that is girded with hope. There should be a love which conveys the fact that we do not have all the answers, but is a love which involves a continual questioning and commitment to constantly deepening experiences. The strength of such love carries a hope and patience which says without words, "Let us wait and see."

21

Loving Mate Number Two, Three, or Nine (Marital Infidelity)

*In vain do they talk of happiness
who have never subdued an impulse
in obedience to a principle.
He who never sacrificed a present
to a future good, or a personal good
to a general good, can speak of happiness
only as the blind speak of colors. (Horace Mann)*

We regard it as one of the laws of mathematics that there are values which have a negative quality. That is, numbers which have a minus sign before them. But in human actions we are reluctant to admit that there are also minus morals, actions which "cost more than they come to." In the equation of life's total they take away more than they promise to give.

If such minus morals came to us as clearly labeled as the negative numbers to which I am comparing them, we might have fewer divorces and fewer unhappy marriages. New experiences and the "new" romance always come to us in the guise of obvious good. An unhappy wife being given approval, sympathy and understanding from a "new" man too often gives herself to those comforts on the grounds that this is what she has longed for in a marriage gone sour. Romance-filled moments have miraculously returned, or so it seems. Sometimes these relationships sustain the feelings of high romance for an extended period, and this convinces the new pair that they are plainly unique; theirs is love like no other. It is not that a second, third, or ninth romance is necessarily *different* than the first, though participants will claim that this is precisely so! It is simply that each successive romance is given a different *interpretation*.

Looking back on the situations that led to their divorce, people will make out of such circumstances exactly what suits their own purposes. The battered spouse syndrome is a good example of this. However, it must be remembered, that where physical violence takes place between two people we will never see more than "the tip of the iceberg."

Consider that case of the wife who came home to find her drunken husband beating the dog. Very wisely, she left the house. However, when she returned an hour and a half later her indignation knew no bounds. To think he would beat a defenseless dog! She claims that she was silent, but reports that she, too, was beaten. It was the very evidence she had wanted long before any beating had taken place. For years she had wanted out. Was her husband, a supercontrolled man when sober, lashing out at what he must have sensed for years? Was the dog merely a "displacement" for his wife in his state of liquid confusion?

Much of the physical violence we are "accepting" in our television shows and in our homes might be changed if it could be shown that happiness does not have to depend on circumstances. Our own reactions and responses to circumstances are what really count.

What escapes us as individuals, and as a nation, is that we can *choose* our own reactions! We are entirely too accepting of the idea that humans are basically violent. Both international conflicts and marital fights are rationalized as justified responses. Instead, politically and individually, conflicts lay the foundations for further violence. The fact that conflicts of any sort leave no one victorious is considered irrational. We accept distortions as a kind of norm. The "right" to express our hostilities and angers is important to our modern culture. To repress or suppress such feelings is to be a phony! To yield is to lay oneself open to added insults.

A comical parallel to the idea of yielding is seen every day on the highways. A driver sees the approaching sign, "YIELD RIGHT OF WAY." It does not occur to him that there is any weakness in giving in at such a juncture; it is simply a matter of mutual survival, a matter of saving one's car! Is a car more valuable than our children, our marriages, our encounters with unreasonable people? To yield is not weakness, but strength! Give the hot tempered person his "right" to explode. Just be aware of the contagion such people generate. It is not easy to refrain from reacting in kind, yet the very resolve not to react places the emphasis on oneself. In such an act, much indignation is deflected away from the provoking situation, and one becomes self-involved in a good sense. Consider Proverbs 16:32, stating that he who rules his spirit is better than he who rules a city.

The fact that Freud has taken suppression and repression as central to his views of sex, and society has made a "taboo" of any and all repressions, does not negate the fact that there are healthy repressions. To be consciously angry and suppress it voluntarily is a thoroughly beneficial discipline. Energy that would be dissipated in the dead ends of angry violence would be made available for other pursuits. The conscious awareness of our own anger can be a powerful incentive for action in other areas.

Another aspect to consider in multiple marriage is that human faculty for being a "double" of oneself. As Thoreau has said, "I only know myself as a human entity; the scene, so to speak, of thoughts and affections, and am sensible of a certain doubleness by which I can stand as remote from myself as from another. However intense my experience, I am conscious of the presence and criticism of a part of me, which , as it were, is not a part of me, but spectator, sharing no experience, but taking note of it; and that is no more I than it is you."

In divorce, this "doubleness" is multiplied according to the mates with which one enters the one-flesh relationship. It is the one form of intimacy by which a person "sins against his *own* flesh." It can be a plague that permits no inner peace, and can be seen in the pursuit of new experiences which such people evidence. The inability to be alone, the avoidance of solitude, the restless search for variety on many levels, the struggle to find a life in externals are all *faces* of the inner dissatisfaction generated by illicit sex. For the once-married, there is a hunger and need that are wholly natural, and yet they transmit themselves so that a preying male can sense it in a woman, just as a woman's intuition informs her of the prowling "wolf."

Consider the case of Mr. and Mrs. Braye and Mr. and Mrs. Bill Jackson. (The names have been changed, but the experience is true.) Mr. Braye had employed a secretary of superior ability as well as outstanding beauty. He was not surprised when she married his law partner, even though it broke up his partner's home. In the mind of Mr. Braye divorce or broken homes were the business of the principals involved. Two children were born to the new couple, and Bill Jackson's children by his previous marriage were frequent visitors. Also, the families of Mr. and Mrs. Braye and the Jacksons were often together socially.

One evening, Mr. and Mrs. Braye were soundly sleeping when their doorbell rang. It was Helen Jackson, his former secretary. With all her previous professionalism, she apologized for her late intrusion, stating that her interruption was most urgent. At this point her self-control wavered, and she blurted out, "Can you lend me five hundred dollars?" Mr. Braye glanced at the clock noting it was 11:45 P.M., and said in startled tones, "Now?"

Helen replied, "Yes, there is a night flight to Caneel Bay, and I must find Bill."

"Wait a minute! Hold on!" interrupted Mr. Braye. "If Bill is in Caneel Bay, he can jolly well come back the same way he went."

"But you don't understand!" cried Helen, "He's not there on business!"

"Are you suggesting he has left you?"

"Worse than that, Mr. Braye, he is there with June Zell, the secretary you hired to replace me," said Helen in despairing tones.

"But how can you be sure?" replied Mr. Braye.

"I know, because that is where he took me, and he boasts of being a creature of habit."

It took several hours for Mr. Braye to dissuade Helen from flying to her husband. Yet, just as Bill Jackson had done five years previously with Helen, events revealed that the pattern was repeated with June Zell, who later became his third wife.

This true account is not to suggest that every second or third marriage is dramatically identical, but in *every* marriage the first flush of romance with a capital "R" takes on a dailiness which is not unlike a fire. The blaze ultimately dies down to a steady flame. Those vibrating thrills "die of their own too much." True, the thrills may be reproduced, but the first excitement cannot last. It is this exhilaration, this intoxication that humans look for when they "fall in love" a second, third or ninth time. These are feelings which can be caught, but never kept. With each repetition, the passing nature of thrills is revealed.

Frank and honest couples will often admit ruefully, 'If I had worked as hard at my first marriage as I do now, we would never have been divorced." The key word is "worked." This is a first requirement despite the romantic nonsense that happiness merely happens. That there is a mysterious "chemistry" to falling in love is a euphemism for the affinity and appetite of glandular attraction—simple biological urge. St. Paul honored it sufficiently to say, "It is better to marry than to burn." There is often a genuine affinity between two people in love, but much more than "chemistry" is involved, and St. Paul spends more time on commitment than he does on the biology of marriage.

We need only look at couples married three, four or more times, famous people whose intelligence is proved by their achievements, to know that there must be a serious gap between intellect which governs a career successfully, but cannot govern its own emotional commitments with any degree of permanence. Of course, we must not forget that many of the much-married famous do not want or seek a life-commitment. What can be learned from the example of the successful businessman or knowledgeable doctor and lawyer or other professional man or woman is that achievement and intelligence are no guarantee of expertise in the emotional arenas of their lives. It has been said of one of this world's wisest men, that his seven hundred wives contributed to the disillusionment of one of his most famous lines: "Futility of futilities, all is futile."

The safest touchstone for participants in any "new" sexual relationship is to note with extreme caution that all everyday behavior is repetitious. If a man or woman is untrue to a first partner, they will also be untrue to the next. It is useless to cite the fact, "But this time it is different!" The difference lies only in a *new perception*. There is great safety from the agony of broken commitments in believing that "The human heart is deceitful above all things."

To those who *want* a permanent commitment, there is no safer way than to assent to God's way. "Let not loyalty and faithfulness forsake you; bind them about your neck, write them on the tablet of your heart. So you will find favor and good repute [Hebrew, understanding] in the sight of God and man. Trust in the LORD with all your heart and do not rely on your own insight. In all your ways acknowledge him, and he will make straight your paths" (Prov. 3:3-5, RSV).

Will such a person be freed from the deceitfulness of his own heart? No, God does not want a blind obedience. We do not "follow cunningly devised fables." Such persons are often shown through painful experiences the depth of the heart's deceitfulness. We are commanded, "Know thyself," and it is frequently a necessary part of our emotional education to attain self-knowledge (much as a child learns to walk) through frequent falls.

But again, it will prove itself true in the most practical of experiences that "The steps of a good man are ordered by the LORD. . . . Though he fall, he shall not be utterly cast down: for the LORD upholdeth him with his hand" (Ps. 37:23-24). We may ask if the Lord will actually do this. And the wayward heart will always reply, "Yes. My heart and life have told me that where I would have grasped a stone, *You* gave me bread!"

"Where the thing we freely forfeit is kept with fonder a
care,
Fonder a care kept than we could have kept it . . ."
Gerard Manley Hopkins, *The Golden Echo*

22

The Unaging Intellect

Every man should use his intellect,
not as he uses his lamp in the study,
only for his own seeing, but as the
lighthouse uses its lamps, that those
afar off on the sea may see the shining,
and learn their way. (H.W. Beecher)

Though it is suggested in "Rabbi Ben Ezra's" monologue that our joys might well be "three-parts pain," we are nonetheless greeted in the same poem with that startlingly optimistic line: "Grow old along with me!/The best is yet to be,/The last of life, for which the first was made."

If we know our Browning, we know that he relied on many characters in whose dramatic utterances he found a vehicle for self-revelation. But now, an entire era has been given over to the worship of youth and one growing old is timid about claims to anything that could remotely be called "best." Like it or not, our youth orientation has not been without certain externally bracing effects. With or without cosmetics or even cosmetic surgery, the sixty-year-old of today appears younger than his counterpart of the same age twenty years ago, yet it is the concern of this essay to explore a far more life-changing aspect of growing old than the removal of jowls or wrinkles.

What was that yet to be "best" to which Browning referred? Is not "best" too large a claim to make for those of us who know that growing old brings all the failing powers that were foretold by the ancients? We cannot deny that dimness of the eyes, afflicted by cataracts or bifocals. We cannot ignore those "grinders" commonly known as false teeth. We are aware of waking at dawn even when we are deaf to that bird-chorus of sunrise. Yes, we have a natural fear of falling where once we felt secure under the slim support of mountain climbing pitons! Where, then, is that "best" in growing old?

Our "best" lies in two alternatives. First, when the outward man decays, the inner man can be renewed. Of course, it must not be supposed that this takes place automatically. Inner renewal is not a shield which compensates for physical decline. The inner man is, after all, the inner resident of a physically deteriorating body and inner renewal will have no effect on the old man or the old woman whose mirror dramatizes a new wrinkle or balding head to which they have attached inordinate importance. To digress briefly, the entire focus of visual barriers in our views of racial differences and the ragged blue-jean cult of our youth zeroes in on this false emphasis on externals. Our "best" lies in the recognition that for too long we have subscribed to that phony dictum, "The apparel oft proclaims the man." Meantime, our way of life ignores the fact that our chief concern should be for the inner self. Now, if external "bests" require the services of the cosmetologist, dermatologist, opthalmologist and the "gist" of scores of "how-to" volumes, much more is required for that inner "best." Indeed, the concept of a healthy mind in a healthy body *begins* with the mind. Perhaps one of our earliest psychosomatic diagnoses is contained in the words, "As a man thinketh in his heart so is he." The chemical components of physical and mental well-being are too well known to review here, for we know that evil thoughts can cause a chemical imbalance. Negativistic, bitter, despairing, discouraged thinking indulged in over a period of time is, in very fact, that "root of bitterness" by which many become defiled (Heb. 12:15, RSV).

Unfortunately, thoughts are not so easily changed. The despairing thought cannot always be willed away, but it can be replaced by the steady, concentrated, day-by-day, search, yes, struggle, for ideas strong enough to displace the self-negating thoughts, which, in essence, any despairing thought becomes. In this process, which psychologists refer to as "displacement," we are given a wide latitude: "Whatsoever things are true, whatsoever things are honest, whatsoever things are just, whatsoever things are pure, whatsoever things are lovely, whatsoever things are of good report; if there be any virtue; and if there be any praise, think on these things" (Phil. 4:8). It is precisely at the word *think* that we move to our second alternative on which old age can fasten its hopes for that promised "best." When we are young we do not recognize how much youthful happiness depends on happenings. Or, as Yeats expresses it, in *Sailing to Byzantium*, "The young. . . caught in that sensual music all neglect/monuments of unaging intellect." Our second alternative promises: "Be ye transformed by the renewing of your mind" (Rom. 12:2). Is this limited to old people? Of course not! However, it is the only area in earthly living where old age can find a "best" that surpasses youth, not by reason of superiority, but by reason of limitation. No longer caught in the cross-currents of sensuality, no longer held, as St. Augustine phrases it, "by the toy of toys." From the "other" side of youth, release from sensuality is not a limitation; it is a freedom. It is a liberty we did not expect to test—whether a renewed mind is indeed a transforming power.

Being persuaded that inner change is possible, how do we proceed? We must not be misled into thinking a fixed formula exists. We cannot ritualistically repeat beautiful platitudes, mystic phrases, or some psychological jargon of positivism, and arrive at a renewed mind. Repetition is never renewal. Moreover, there is no arrival; there is *continual* transformation and *continual* becoming. It is a process, for renewal implies process and change. If there is transformation and renewal, then it follows there is also anticipation. Try to remember what anticipation did to us in youth! The power of magnifying either calamity or joy is a terrifying human attribute except where it fastens its abilities to happy expectations. But by expectation I do not mean some specific wish-fulfillment or Mencken's pie-in-the-sky piety; I mean a world-encompassing sense of God's goodness following us all the days of our lives. Such anticipation is not a false fancy when it is harnessed to the very practical goal of renewing our minds. It was to this that Yeats also gave his assent when he wrote, "An aged man is but a paltry thing,/A tattered coat upon a stick,/Unless Soul clap its hands and sing."

23

The Invisible Partnership:
Enduring Marriage

As are families, so is society. (Thayer)

Paradoxically, no age preceding the twentieth century has upheld the importance of personal autonomy to the degree that modern man does. But for the believer in man's invisible partnership with God, autonomy as a way of life must be relinquished. Such a one must accept the humiliation of his unbelieving contemporaries by agreeing with their judgment of him. When union with God is described in the following words from Scripture, even atheists agree. ". . . Not many wise, . . . not many noble, are called." Thus far all readers agree, but the end of that line requires the patience and humiliation of faith: ". . . not many wise, . . . not many noble, are called: *But God hath chosen the foolish [weak] things of the world to confound the wise*" (1 Cor. 1:26, 27; italics mine).

Moreover, since our union with God is a passive union, we do not choose Him. We are chosen, or caused to choose Him. "Ye have not chosen me, but I have chosen you." Through Christ, the Light of the world, we transcend ourselves, and become partakers of His wisdom, since He promises, "Christ is made unto us wisdom. . . ." This is the invisible partnership that *must* undergird and support the human institution of marriage. It follows that it is not in *any* qualities of the marriage partner that the endurance and safety of the marriage union depends, *for each partner is human*. Enduring marriage survives through enduring love, yet what human is capable of enduring love? "The human heart is deceitful above all things, and who can know it?" Only from that union described as the "obscurity of faith," can human love transcend itself. Only then, can human love take to itself the claim, "For love is strong as death."

Deathless love then, is not of that cinematic variety portrayed for us on stage and screen, nor is sexual compatibility its hallmark! Moreover, it cannot be conditional or circumstantial, for this is to "risk" an endurance based on change, and such a base can never be anything but contradictory or fluctuating. The love that endures places *principles above personalities!*

The overbalancing importance attached to the physical is clearly shown in current trends, where more and more couples live together in the one-flesh relationship without ceremony or commitment (other than private). If the sexual attraction endures they may call it love, and having proved it to their own satisfaction, may seal the union with the appropriate legal sanction. But the practice remains a sad commentary on the supremacy of glandular preference. If it is true of an unchurched majority that glands dictate the evaluation of a relationship, it is even more tragic when Christians are smitten with the same contagion. Spoken bluntly, many believers explain their divorces by saying, "I could never go to bed with anyone for whom I have lost all feeling." The key word is *feeling*. Rather than try to change the *cause* of lost feeling, emotions are allowed to trigger irreversible situations. Meantime, the real issue is not sexual compatibility, but a pervasive, overall immaturity, for an inability to feel for one's mate is often related to a long list of immature reactions in every area of life.

The alarming increase in extra-marital affairs is merely one single facet of a decadence that extends to our national preoccupation with "instant" satisfactions, whether that be food, amusement, education, friendships, material advancement, or politics. The invisible partners in good marital sex are not of the "instant" variety; they are honesty, understanding, loyalty, consideration, forgiveness, and a "plain vanilla" quality we call affection. There is no list of rules for enduring marriage, no recipe of so-called "mature" qualities that will provide "how-to" instructions. Too many golden-year marriages have survived such incompatibilities as no matched interests, few complementary psychological needs, and totally unequal stages of personality development. Why? Because each partner in such examples of marital "imbalance" overbalanced the imbalance with individuality that was no threat to endurance.

We should remind ourselves that in the greatest "imbalance" that any marriage can encounter, namely, the marriage of believers with unbelievers, St. Paul gave God the majority rule.
". . . If any brother hath a wife
that believeth not,
and she be pleased to dwell with him,
let him not put her away.
And the woman which hath an husband
that believeth not,
and if he be pleased to dwell with her,
let her not leave him.
For the unbelieving husband

is sanctified by the wife,
and the unbelieving wife
is sanctified by the husband:
else were your children unclean;
but now are they holy."
(1 Cor. 7:12-14)